$\int$PIRIT $\mathcal{G}$UIDES and

$\mathcal{A}$NGELS

*How I Communicate
with Heaven*

KEVIN HUNTER

WARRIOR
OF LIGHT
PRESS

Warrior of Light Press
www.kevin-hunter.com

Body, Mind & Spirit/Angels & Guides
Inspiration & Personal Growth

PRODUCTION CREDITS:
Project Editor: James Szopo

Content in *Spirit Guides and Angels* is taken from the books,
Warrior of Light: Messages from my Guides and Angels,
Empowering Spirit Wisdom, *Realm of the Wise One* and *Darkness
of Ego*.

Acknowledgements

Thank you to my spiritual posse that consists of God and my personal sports team of Angels, Guides, Archangels and Saints.

WARRIOR OF LIGHT
POCKET BOOK SERIES

♥

Chapters

A Word

Spirit Guides and Angels is a mini-pocket book and part of a series of Warrior of Light books. Some of the content in the mini-pocket books are disbursed throughout three of the bigger Warrior of Light books called: Warrior of Light: Messages from my Guides and Angels, Empowering Spirit Wisdom and Darkness of Ego. The exception is the book, The Seven Deadly Sins. The bigger Warrior of Light books contain a variety of information within the spiritual empowerment genre. The reason behind releasing five separate mini-pocket books is for those who just want to read about one specific topic and are not interested in the rest. For example, all content soul mate love and relationship related would be in the mini-pocket book called, Soul Mates and Twin Flames. Rather than having to buy all three big books to read about the information in each of them, you have it all in one mini-pocket book.

Author's Note

All *Warrior of Light* books are infused with practical messages and guidance that my Spirit team has taught and shared with me revolving around many different topics. The main goal is to fine tune your body, mind and soul. This improves humanity one person at a time. You are a Divine communicator and perfectly adjusted and capable of receiving messages from Heaven. This is for your benefit in order to live a happier, richer life. It is your individual responsibility to respect yourself and this planet while on your journey here.

The messages and information enclosed in this and all of the *Warrior of Light* books may be in my own words, but they do not come from me. They come from God, the Holy Spirit, my Spirit team of guides, angels and sometimes certain Archangels and Saints. I am merely the liaison or messenger in delivering and interpreting the intentions of what they wish to communicate. They love that I talk about them and share this stuff as it gets other people to work with them too!

There is one main hierarchy Saint who works with me leading the pack. His name is Nathaniel. He is often brutally truthful and forceful, as he does not mince words. There may be topics in this and my other books that might bother you or make you uncomfortable. He asks that you examine the underlying cause of this discomfort and come to terms with the fear attached. He cuts right to the heart of humanity without apology. I have learned quite a bit from him while adopting his ideology, which is Heaven's philosophy as a whole.

I am one with the Holy Spirit and have many Spirit Guides and Angels around me. As my connections to the other side grew to be daily over the course of my life, more of them joined in behind the others. I have often seen, sensed, heard and been privy to the dozens of magnificent lights that crowd around me on occasion.

If I use the word "He" when pertaining to God, this does not mean that I am advocating that he is a male. Simply replace the word, "He" with one you are comfortable using to identify God for you to be. This goes for any gender I use as examples. When I say, "spirit team", I am referring to a team of 'Guides and Angels'. The purpose of the *Warrior of Light* books is to empower and help you improve yourself, your life and humanity as a whole. It does not matter if you are a beginner or well versed in the subject matter. There may be something that reminds you of something you already know or something that you were unaware of. We all have much to share with one another, as we are all one in the end. This book and all of the *Warrior of Light* series of books contain information and directions on how to reach the place where you can be a fine tuned instrument to receive your own messages from your own Spirit team.

Some of my personal stories are infused and sprinkled in the books. This is in order for you to see how it works effectively for me. With some of my methods, I hope that you gain insight, knowledge or inspiration. It may prompt you to recall incidents where you were receiving heavenly messages in your own life. There are helpful ways that you can improve your existence and have a connection with Heaven throughout this book. Doing so will greatly transform yourself in all ways allowing you to attract wonderful circumstances at higher levels and live a happier more content life.

~ Kevin Hunter

Spirit Guides and Angels

Chapter One

SPIRIT GUIDES AND ANGELS

How often do you find yourself thinking about nothing in particular when suddenly a jolt of clear-cut information flies through your mind? What you receive is so commanding you experience a surge of uplifting joy coursing through all of the cells in your body. The idea, key or answer you gained was the missing piece of the puzzle to something you needed to know at that particular time. How many times have you received a nudge to do something that would positively change your life? Instead of taking action on it, you deny it chalking it off to wishful thinking. You later discover that it was indeed an answered prayer, if only you had taken notice and followed the guidance. These are some examples of how you can tell when it is your Spirit Guide or Guardian Angel communicating with you. When you get your lower self and ego out of the way, then that is when the profound answer you had been hoping for is revealed to you. The impression you acquire is so powerful that it pulls you out of the darkness you were previously stuck in. It is a bright light shining its focus directly onto the message in unadorned view. It is crystal clear as if it had been there all along and you wonder why you had not noticed it before.

There are so many joyless faces out there waiting, complaining or praying for a miracle. Instead you choose to fill your days up partaking in activities that only erode your self-esteem and overall well-being. These activities can be something you are not aware of such as sitting in traffic completely tense. You experience another mundane routine day screaming for an escape from this prison of a life you have created. You stay unhappy in your jobs, the places you live in and with certain friendships or relationships. You ponder over not having that home of your dreams or sharing your life with someone in a loving relationship. The days having this dull mindset turn into months and years with no miracle in sight. This disappointment grows like mold causing you to appear and feel eternally glum, negative and bitter. The emotional traits mask your dissatisfaction and heartbreak attracting more of that stuff to you. To cope you drown those nasty emotions with addictions from drinking heavily, ingesting chemicals, doing drugs or by partaking in time wasting activities such as gossip and Internet surfing.

You choose to be disconnected living behind a wall built of your own attitude and yet it is in your basic human nature to want to connect to other human souls, to someone, or something. You want to be happy, but that state can feel so out of reach and unobtainable you drown in its thoughts. Our way of communicating today is primarily through phone, texting, email and social networking. Even if you truly wanted to sit face-to-face you are too busy or worn out to bother. You were not intended to live your life in misery and unhappiness. For some reason, you choose to fall into a pattern of suffering. Human souls as a whole are to blame for this design.

It is never too late to improve your life. What you are looking for is right in front of you and closer than you think. Strengthen your faith and believe in the power of what exists outside of your human body. This will bring you closer to the happiness that resides within. God, your angels, spirit guides and all in Heaven can and want to assist you out of this hopelessness. They are always present around you. They want to lift you out of your life of desolation. It is irrelevant what your beliefs are and whether you are religious or an atheist. It does not matter what race you were born into in this lifetime. Nor does it matter if you are rich or poor, gay or straight, liberal or conservative. Whatever you agreed to come into this lifetime as, you are loved equally. No one is more special than anyone else. God and the angels see each of your inner lights, your innocence and your true purpose for being here. If you have veered long off course, they can help you get back to where you need to be. Who you are is a perfect child of God and love no matter where you are from or who you are.

A Spirit Guide once lived as a human soul, but a Guardian Angel has always been a Spirit. Every human soul has one Spirit Guide and one Guardian Angel assigned to work with them throughout their entire Earthly life. They are your immediate army that works with you daily. This is from the moment you were born until you pass on to the next life. They know everything about you, from your thoughts and feelings, to your wants and desires. Murderers, serial killers and those filled with hate towards other human souls also have one Spirit Guide and one Guardian Angel with them. Because you have free will choice, those human souls are not listening to or following the guidance that is passed onto them by their Spirit team.

Your personal Spirit team is anyone on the other side you work with regularly. Since everyone is assigned at least one Spirit Guide and one Guardian Angel from birth until death, then that is your Spirit team. Some human souls have more than one Spirit Guide and one Guardian Angel, if you have been requesting additional assistance from Heaven, or you are working with angels on a daily basis. These Guides and Angels are attracted to your light and know if you are an honorable person. They can see how bright your light shines. The brighter your light is, the more attracted they are to you and may then come to your side. They know you are one with Heaven and are excited to work with you and help you along your journey. Some may come to you simply to protect you. Others may come to you in order to assist you with an important task. Once that task has been accomplished, then that Guide or Angel leaves to help someone else. Meanwhile your one main Spirit Guide and Guardian Angel never leave until you cross over where you will come face to face with them.

Your Spirit team does not make your choices for you. They work with you to help you along with your spiritual growth and to keep you on the right path. They assist in orchestrating circumstances that will improve your life when it is time. This can include coming into contact with particular people on Earth to help enhance your life in some way, or to teach you certain lessons or gain specific knowledge. You can call on your Spirit team to assist you at anytime. You do have to personally ask for their assistance because they cannot intervene with your free will. They may stand idly around while you make one mistake after another. They are unable to interfere with your poor choices unless you have asked them to or permanently invited them in. They will attempt to get your attention if you are heading off your life path, but they cannot stop you. They know that these mistakes you make are essential to your spiritual growth.

When you make mistakes and bad things

continuously happen for you, then this is a wakeup call. These situations are getting you to notice the negative synchronistic pattern, and to stop the cycle and find another path. Your Guides and Angels hope that it will wake you up to say, *"Wait a minute. What am I doing? Obviously, the way I have been living has not been entirely successful. Guides and Angels, I call upon you now. Please work with me by guiding me down the right path. Help me to reach a place of peace. Thank you."*

You are always receiving Guardian Angel and Spirit Guide communication, messages and nudges, but are you paying attention to them?

More people than not believe in angels regardless of what their spiritual beliefs are. God, Heaven and the Angels are all non-denominational. This means that they do not belong to any religious sect. You can be a non-believer and they are still with you, working with you and guiding you.

Your Spirit Guide and Guardian Angel are with you from the time you are born until you exit this life. Your Spirit Guide is typically a deceased relative, but not always. This deceased relative is one who has chosen to be your Spirit Guide before you were born. It can even be a relative from centuries back! This Spirit Guide has gone through formal training to be able to efficiently guide you. They know when not to interfere and to allow you free will choice. If they see that you are a danger to yourself or someone else, they will tap you on the shoulder and attempt to divert your attention.

Let's use an extreme story and say that you decide to head over to someone's house to do drugs all night. Your Spirit Guide will nudge you to head down another course. Your ego is so strong and powerful that it will convince you that you will be happier if you go into that house and get high. What might end up happening can be a circumstance that propels you into the bell jar. An array of negative activity can follow such as you experience an overdose, someone steals your wallet, something medically goes wrong or you have an accident. Perhaps you lose your job, a friendship, relationship or any other incident that thrusts your life into a downward spiral preceding that night. From this one incident, you attract in more of the same causing you to experience one detriment after another further delaying your life purpose. Your Spirit Guide cannot stop you, but they are communicating with you in an attempt to get you to notice a different life choice that will not have such negative repercussions. This is the extent of the intervention since they are not allowed to stop you from doing that drug unless it results in death before your time. Even then, many human souls under the influence of drugs or alcohol rarely listen to their Spirit team. There are cases where your guides did all they can do and were unable to divert you from continued bad behavior. You were not paying attention, but instead consumed in pain, greed or rebelliousness, which results in your early death.

Your Spirit Guide and Guardian Angel may alternate with specific roles in helping you. When you are down or depressed, your Guardian Angel may be the one that tries to get your attention to focus on the bright side of life. They will caress and soothe your heart Chakra relieving you of any heavy burdens you might be feeling. Your Guardian Angel will be the one that works with you on your feelings of well-being, prompting you to be more optimistic and joyful. Your Spirit Guide will work with you on practical matters with you that lead you to the job or career you always wanted. Your Spirit Guide may direct you to take certain classes in the area of your dream making sure you stick to it. This is followed by the job that is beneficial for you at that time, even if it is not quite the job you always wanted. Sometimes you have to go through your own individual training and lessons with several different jobs before you are shown the big dream job. They do not give you anything immediately necessarily, but they gradually guide you towards your dream goal in steps.

You could be someone who has spent years looking for a job only to be met with distress that there is no work out there. There may be times where there are no jobs in your chosen area of interest. You are guided to take a particular job, but you do not notice it since it is not the job you want. You are being expected to start somewhere even in a position you do not want. You may be asked to take a position that you feel is beneath you or for less pay. I have done this myself only to find that it leads directly to the dream position I do want. I am suddenly catapulted upwards towards one of the greatest jobs I would have had to date. You need to have faith and understand that there is a divine plan for you.

All those in Heaven are present in this Earthly life to make your life easier, but the catch is that you have to ask them for help, as they cannot intervene without your consent. The only time they do intercede is when there is a life-threatening situation before it's your time to go. This is God's law as he gave you an ego and free will. Ego and free will are the biggest cause of turmoil, hate and destruction known to man. You are given free will choice to either live in peace or live stressed out. Which one would you like to have?

You can have more peace and joy in your life when you start paying attention to your Spirit team's guidance. They do not live your life for you because you are here to learn and grow. However, they do assist you in navigating gracefully out of circumstances that consistently cause you grief, stress and depression. They do not want you to suffer, but you must learn valuable lessons while here on Earth.

I made great strides and shifts from living under duress with a wide range of addictions to living more at peace by working with my Spirit team. Your Spirit Guide and Guardian Angel help improve your soul. They can help you have more time available, to getting more exercise, or to finding the right job. For some circumstances, the change is immediate. For bigger needs, it may take much longer. This is because there are pieces of the puzzle that they must maneuver around on your behalf. You may not be quite ready for what is to come. You have additional life lessons to learn before you graduate to the next step. Everything is all set according to divine timing, but if you do not ask your Spirit team for help, then they stand by watching you suffer. They watch you feel needlessly miserable when all you need to do is call out to them. I liken it to the mythological stories about Vampires that state that a Vampire cannot enter your house unless you invite it in. This concept is similar to asking anyone in Heaven or the Spirit world for assistance. They will stand outside your door waiting patiently for you to say the magic words and invite them into your life. It is like having a winning sports team on your side, as you cannot lose!

I have always believed in angels and have never questioned Heaven's existence. I do not falsely follow something without testing it out first. I have an analytical mind that questions everything and is suspicious of anything. When I receive proof or a response that validates what I am questioning, then I become a believer.

The reason I greatly believe in God, Heaven, the Angels and Spirit Guides is that I have been testing them my entire life. I have had immense feedback and success simply by paying attention to their Divine intervention and communication. I do not try to convince or convert anybody, but rather share information about them to those interested. I will graciously part with some of the messages that they have shared with me throughout my life.

There are those who are deeply religious who have said that you are not supposed to pray to angels or archangels. I have never seen anyone including myself urge anyone to pray to the angels.

Asking your guide and Angel for assistance is not praying to them. They are the gifts from God who are available to help when you need it. They are His arms and hands that connect you to Him. When you are experiencing negative emotions, then you cut yourself off from God. The angels, guides and archangels raise your vibration to the level of happiness so that you feel God's connection. Their role is to lift you to a happier state where you are at peace. This level is where you will feel God's presence and receive His communication. When you ask your Spirit team for help, you are essentially reaching out to God.

Asking them for help is mandatory if you desire assistance in your life. When you are upset or stressed out, not only do you not receive God's wisdom, but you forget to ask for help. All you have to do is ask, whether that be mentally, out loud or even in writing. I have even sent some of them an email. I send it to myself and then I file it away. You can write to them in a journal, notebook or on a piece of paper. It does not matter how you ask for help, or how you word it, or how you say it, since no special invocation is needed. They will move into your vicinity before you have finished your sentence. What is important is having the intention.

For example, you can think something like this, "Okay angels, I need your help with this." The right Guide or Angel has already rushed in before you have finished your sentence. Sometimes they respond immediately, but if it is a complicated issue it may take a bit longer. It is important to have faith and trust that they are and have indeed stepped in, and they are working with you on your concern. Sometimes they may respond in ways that you may not be noticing. After it has hit you a few times you may get that moment where you say, "Okay, I thought something was going on with that." You must be open and receptive knowing that sometimes they may not answer you in the way you are expecting.

My mom taught me how to pray when I was a wee tike. Every night as I went to bed she would enter my room and say my prayers with me. We were not religious and there was not a shred of guilt, fear or damnation surrounding our prayers. Her goal was that we all grow up to be good people helping and contributing to the world in a positive way. We said these prayers every night.

My mom was and is all compassion and love for all people regardless of their interests or lifestyle choices. Her mantra in these prayers was to practice and teach love while in this lifetime when we were young and when we grow up. She would walk me through communicating to Jesus, Mother Mary and Joseph. I never had the fear and guilt when connecting to Jesus or Mother Mary specifically. I did grow up to notice that others did not share these same beliefs.

I had noticed that when I used the words God, Heaven, Jesus or Mother Mary around certain people that they would fidget uncomfortably. Some of that is fear and guilt. They were raised to associate those words with those who speak of an angry, judgmental and negative God. Even if others disagreed, I have never seen Jesus or Mother Mary in any other way than all love. It is important to not be led by human ego. They insist on creating the fear that there is a merciless Heaven that will cast you out into fire and brimstone at any moment. God will never cease to love you, but he does expect you to correct your mistakes and behavior. This is especially true if it is delaying you on your path, and you are hurting yourself or someone else.

You have a life purpose and mission to accomplish while you are here and it is your goal to discover what that is. Everyone needs to be contributing something in a positive way that is bringing love to another person. You were not born angry, bitter and depressed. Other human souls have inflicted that belief system on you. You absorbed it and reacted to it in ways where it might have permanently damaged you. It will be reversed and undone in this life or in the next when you pray and ask for heavenly assistance to lift those burdens off your soul. Invite in Heaven to permanently work with you on improving your life. They love you and want to help you reach a state of peace and contentment in your life.

Chapter Two

How Do Guides and Angels Communicate With You

There are a plethora of spirit beings in many of the heavenly realms that exist. They include angels, guides, archangels, spirit guides, guardian angels, realm spirits, saints, ascended masters and deceased loved ones. Since they cannot just pick up the phone and call you, they use other varying means and methods to communicate with you called *clairs*. Your senses are divine communication tools with Heaven! This is why your senses, Chakras and over all well-being needs to be kept clean of debris and trash that blocks the communication line with God. The more negative you are, then the more clogged your *clairs* get. This is why spiritual practitioners insist on living as joyful and toxic free of a life as you can manage. You are born with naturally heightened clear channels of communication to the other side.

The four basic Clair channels are:

Clairvoyance (clear seeing)
Clairaudience (clear hearing)
Clairsentience (clear feeling)
Claircognizance (clear knowing)

Others have shared stories of children talking to angels or friends that no one else can see. Unfortunately, some adults thrash and shatter that belief in those children by saying, "Oh that's just your imaginary friend." These invented friends are not always as imaginary as a jaded adult might believe.

You are born with heightened functioning clairs, but there are typically one or two clairs that are more dominant in you than others. Over time your clair channels dim and darken due to things such as: Blocks created by society, a heavy interest in the material world, domination of your ego, consumption of negative substances, and poor lifestyle choices. These are some of the predominant situations that clog your clair channels. When your clair channels are clogged, then this prevents you from communicating or even knowing that you are receiving messages from Heaven.

CLAIRAUDIENCE

Clairaudience means "clear hearing". You are hearing the voices of Heavenly messages and guidance being filtered through what is called your Ear Chakra. For as long as I can remember, I have heard voices from the spirit world in my left ear as guidance and messages. The voices of my Guides and Angels are clear as if they are standing next to me talking into an ear that has been deafer than the other since birth. When I was four years old, my Mother had taken me to the Doctor for repeated hearing checkups. She had later told me that I was not responding to any of the tests in one of my ears. Therefore they thought I might be fully deaf in that ear. The sounds of the outside world are fainter in that ear than the other. Instead the volume is cranked up to the spirit world in the deafer ear. Every now and then I hear a ringing in that ear. This has been undetected by medical professionals to be anything of concern. This is my Spirit team downloading important and vital information for me that I would need to access at some point. I equate it to hooking up a flash drive to your computer and moving important files off it and onto your hard drive for immediate access. At times, I will hear a dial up internet sound in my inner ear as if it is trying to connect. Other times if the reception is not clear, it will sound as if I am switching the channels on a radio station until I hear a clear song.

Music is and has always been my escape. I love

music as I am a rocker after all, but that is the only area I prefer it loud. As a clairaudient, I hear the heavenly inspiration and messages carried on the notes of music. This is where I hear everything clearly. All other loud sounds and noises are intrusive and strictly shunned and forbidden around me. This includes things such as crowd noise, sirens, airplanes, trashcans banging, screaming of any kind. Unpleasant noises are incredibly heightened and uncomfortable. I hear footsteps around me or someone approaching and I immediately know who is coming or what type of person they are. I figured I was odd in that I constantly fixated on what others deemed to be an unimportant sound. These are signs of someone having a higher level of clairaudience.

I put my spark and passion into my writing projects. I hear the music and the rhythms and that is how my Spirit team communicates with me. I hear it in the notes, in the music, in people's conversations, in the line at the store and it inspires me. I tap into the waves of the ocean and the voices rush over that and through the white noise. The music translates into verbal messages coming through the sounds and inspiration.

I hear everything in the sounds, from people's voices, to the patterns in people's footsteps. I can tell what people are up to from those sounds. As a child, I thought I was just a spaz having an acute hearing ability to every sound that happens around me. I did not know until adulthood that there was an actual word for it called *clairaudience*.

One afternoon I was running late and I could

not find my car keys anywhere. I started throwing everything around in a panic mentally shouting, "Where are my keys!"

I huffed and puffed throwing items all over the place in a panic. I shouted again, "Angels. Where are my keys?!"

I heard a loud male voice in my left ear shout, "On your bed!!" Without hesitating, I charged into the bedroom. There were my keys on the bed sitting all alone. I grabbed them abruptly and headed towards my car. I mentally repeated the words to my Spirit team, "Thank you. Thank you. Thank you." Heaven is unfazed by your sudden upset. All they see is the love buried inside you. This does not give one license to behave as I did, but as you work with them more, you are less hostile and more appreciative. They see the light within you and ignore the range of wasted emotions, because to them everything is all right.

As my interest in the spiritual crowd grew, I wanted to know what they were like since I never believed I fit into any group. I went to an all day spiritually based convention to be around like-minded souls. While there, I would agree to give someone a cold reading in the audience. This was not a test, but an exercise using no divination tool such as oracle or tarot cards. I personally did not need them even though part of me enjoyed double-checking and confirming the messages through those tools. This is where the angels reminded me once again as they do repeatedly with all of us, "TRUST." Having to do a cold read in a space with hundreds of people's energies around me while on little sleep was not my cup of tea. I wanted to bolt out of there at lightning speed and crawl back into bed. I knew there was no way out. I could feel my team pushing me out of my comfort zone. I would need a volunteer to participate in this exercise.

A young girl who was sitting near me raised her hand and said she will do the read with me. She pulled her chair to face me and closed her eyes. I reached my hand out around her head to feel the air pressure energy. My Spirit team said that this was not about me. This is about this girl in front of me. I closed my eyes and took several deep breaths until I was relaxed.

I called in my Spirit team and said, "Please get my ego out of the way. This is about this girl right here. It is all about her and not me. If anyone would like to come through for her, please come forward now."

I repeated those words with my eyes closed waiting in stillness for some communication in any form. I heard a male voice speak loud and clear through my clairaudience channel. My ego was naturally trying to make me second-guess it. I opened my eyes and what I said stopped her:

"There is a pleasant man who is around you right now. He says he is always with you. He is telling me that his name is Ralph. He is your grandfather. He has been working closely with you on your education and towards your life purpose."

When I noticed the girl's eyes flooded with tears I stopped talking. She informed me that she is sixteen years old and in High School. I thought she was in her early twenties as she had a mature look to her. She carried herself confidently as if she were an adult. She was also at this conference alone. She said her Mother's Dad, her Grandfather, died when she was seven years old. She then said that his name was "RALPH".

Most of the time you are getting accurate information and messages from your own Spirit team, but you discredit it or talk yourself out of it being real. I heard a male voice clearly telling me his name for this young girl. I thought I was imagining it at first. I was thinking, "I don't know any Ralph. This is silly." My Spirit team prompted me to trust in the communication I was getting and not second guess it. It may not mean anything to me, but it might mean something to someone else. I bit the bullet and decided to tell the girl what I heard knowing that I might be wrong. This was an excellent case where I realized again that there are loved ones communicating with you in Heaven. This was a complete stranger whom I had never met. Nor had I known anything about her. Yet, I told her about her deceased grandfather. I am not a working Medium, but what I did in that instance for that girl was what one would call, *Mediumship*. This is something anyone can do if they work at it. Do not doubt or second-guess the messages you receive. Do not worry if you make a mistake. To do so is operating from your imposter lower self or ego.

All psychics read in a variety of different ways. Not everyone has the same gifts. For example, some will need to have the person in front of them to read them, while others need to have them on the phone to hear their voice vibration or to pick up on their energy. I do not need to see or hear the person. I am too sensitive to every nuance around me that I have found it to be more of a distraction at times. I am able to hear the voice of spirit without having the person present. The voices are loud when I'm in a centered state. Sometimes they chime in before someone has finished their sentence.

CLAIRCOGNIZANCE

Claircognizance means "clear knowing". This is receiving heavenly messages and guidance through your crown chakra above your head. I am profoundly claircognizant, which is similar to having a computer in the mind. I receive Divine information through my crown Chakra that later proves to be true. Having claircognizance is when you know the answer to a topic or subject matter that you are not versed in.

I have had others ask, "How did you know that was going to happen?" I would say, "I don't know. I just knew." Growing up when they would ask that question I would stare at them blankly not understanding. I did not know how I knew.

Someone with claircognizance always seems to know when someone is lying to them, even if they don't call them out on it. I would typically keep it to myself unless it is something major that needs addressing. This information proves useful on occasion, but then there are certain things you do not want to know and would prefer to be naïve to. You know this information is passed onto you for a reason. It is to protect you or someone else by saving them time and potential heartache.

A claircognizant would know if someone is cheating on them or on someone else. I have known things about someone from a first meeting and what they are like. I can tell immediately what role they would play in my life if any. Everyone I dated romantically, I knew at first glance that I would be with them soon or in the future. It would later happen and come to fruition. There was no explanation for it and I never questioned it. This is an example of what claircognizance and clear knowing is.

My mind is always on, thinking and working. Sometimes I find it difficult to shut it off when I need it to. I had asked my Doctor once if there was something I could take that would help me to stop thinking specifically at night. He laughed and said, "Unfortunately there isn't anything like that." It was something that I had to accept as a gift and learn to use it to my advantage. Knowing things before they happened and not known how or why has saved my life in many great ways.

Information or guidance comes to you when you are not trying to get it. When you push to receive guidance or messages, then that is when you block it. Your fear is that you will not pick up on any messages, or that the messages you receive are your imagination. As a result, you hear and receive nothing. Second guessing what you're receiving is a block.

Your Spirit team is always communicating with you, but your strong will to try to receive messages can dim the connection. The underlying core reason is due to fear, or destructive and unhelpful self-talk. Negative emotions block communication with the other side. You can ask the angels to remove the blocks that cut off the communication to them. Ask them to help you clearly hear, see, know, and feel the messages they wish to relay to you.

One Summer, I was talking with a group of people standing in a circle at a beach BBQ. There were many huddles of people talking at this BBQ around my group too. As I was talking to them, I took one-step back grabbing the bottle of wine behind me to my right. I proceeded to pour it into the glass of a woman who was in another huddle near my group. She jolted in shock and laughed into a shout. "I was just going to get more wine! Wait! How did you know that? Ok that was weird." I just shrugged and said, "I don't know. I just knew." I had no idea how I knew and I was not looking at the woman or facing her. Something had prompted me to turn, grab the wine and pour. Sometimes the clear knowing is slight and can surround something as insignificant as this.

Other examples of having Claircognizance are where you know the answers to problems or topics you are not educated in, yet you had the right answer that solved it when others were perplexed. People with an analytical mind tend to be claircognizant. They are great problem solvers such as a Scientist or Teacher. Their own Spirit team filters this information through them. Ironically, those with claircognizance tend to be the ones who are skeptical of psychic phenomena. One of the reasons is due to their analytical or scientific mind. They need concrete proof of anything unseen with their physical eyes. Yet, they're receiving heavenly guidance through their claircognizance channel.

I have always been wise beyond my years. In High School, I was the guy who would sit up in the bleachers, and one by one a different student would approach me to divulge their issues as if I were their own private counselor. They were from every different clique you could imagine: the nerd, the jock, the cheerleader, the techie, the bully and the bullied would all come up to me solo at varying intervals. I would say a sentence or two to them that assisted their situation. They would cry out in relief with something along the lines of, "God you always know just what to say!"

They would say things like, "It's as if you're this old soul who knows the answers to life and yet you're a teenager in High School. How do you know so much?"

I knew that I was different, but the majority appreciated this eccentricity. I rarely had an unsettling moment. I did not think of myself as being different just for knowing information, but it was the whole package. I did not follow the crowd and was uninterested in fads or being popular. I never thought of myself as a follower and have always been an independent leader. I am comfortable with being alone and have no desire for a constant demanding need for attention. I did not care if anybody liked or did not like me. My goal was and has always been beyond that. This is also the many marks of what some call a soul of the Indigo Generation.

I was walking past a colleague from a former job in the past. He stopped me and said, "Hey Kevin, I want to ask you a question. What do you think of bacon toothpaste?"

Without flinching or displaying shock I said, "I don't know. That sounds like something someone in Iowa would invent."

His face turned white. "How the Hell did you know that?"

I said, "I don't know."

He proceeds to inform me. "I'm talking to a friend of mine online who is in Iowa and he was just telling me that he's inventing this toothpaste with bacon in it. Okay, Kevin that was weird. How did you know that?"

"I - I don't know. It's just what I thought of."

This is an example of claircognizance in action where you know the accurate answers and do not know how you know. Because this is a regular occurrence for me, I never found it to be appropriate to get into a lengthy explanation with anyone about it. There is no efficient way of explaining how I know something. It appears as if I grabbed it out of thin air. I ignore the question or run over it with something else. As a Claircognizant, I always know just how to respond.

How often have you had the answer to

something you knew nothing about? You may have had that person ask you, 'How did you know that?' You stare at them blankly. "I don't know." This is an example of messages delivered to you through your claircognizance channel.

CLAIRVOYANCE

Clairvoyance means "clear seeing". It is when someone sees moving pictures in their mind's eye. These images might be a premonition of what's to come, what's already happened or is currently happening. This is the most well-known Clair. Once in awhile I see images and moving visuals in my mind's eye or Third Eye Chakra located between your eye brows. Those that have heightened clairvoyance see spirits as if they are standing in front of them. Those spirits are not necessarily whole like you and I, but rather appear opaque or translucent. Other forms of clairvoyance can include prophetic dreams. These images can be of importance to someone's future whether it is a warning or if something good is coming into their life such as a romantic partner or a great job.

As a child, I saw images of people that sometimes appeared scary. Once I saw someone who looked very real leaving my room. My heart beat fast not knowing who or what that was. The next minute I am standing in front of my mother's bed in the dark. Dead tired she asks, "What is it?" Unable to speak, I saw another visual of someone under her bed smiling. Trying to find the right words as a child to communicate that I was pretty sure I was seeing dead people was difficult. I said, "There's someone in the house." She'd say, "There's no one here. It's just your imagination." As a Claircognizant, I did not buy this response. I chose to keep it all to myself from that point forward. I knew I would not get anywhere trying to convince an adult of something that is real and not imaginary.

Clairvoyant messages delivered can come to you in many ways including in your dreams. In a vivid dream, I was wandering through what appeared to be an upper scale mall that one might find in a fancy Las Vegas Hotel. There was a Spirit in a long black robe floating high in the air in the distance. It had a robe hoodie pulled over its skeleton head with hollow eyes. It looked like the "Day of the Dead" artwork that one would find depicted in certain Mexican art. Spotting it and knowing this was no friend, I mumbled, "uh-oh". The Spirit was alerted when I said that and looked right through me. He quickly flew in the air around the gorgeous gold fountain in the center of the mall and headed directly towards me. I turned to run, but in dreams you do not always run, move or get far when being chased. Unable to move I was paralyzed with heaviness and pain. The Spirit landed in front of me pulling out a long spear. He held it up and stabbed me in the stomach with it. The pain was sharp and I sensed every bit of it as I jolted awake. The pain continued after I awoke and then evaporated to a good degree until I felt nothing. It reminded me of the horror movie, "Nightmare on Elm Street". In the movie something bad happens to you in the dream and you take it out feeling it with you as you wake up. I lit some Sage incense leaves to clear my space. Connecting with my guides I discovered that the Spirit was not a demon spirit that I invited in. It was me! It was my fear that manifested that false entity. The Spirit stabbed me in my stomach where your Sacral Chakra is. This is where your power lies. They were explaining that I was giving my power away and needed to take it back. I had to stop with the ego infested fears and worries as they were unfounded. I invoked a white light from the other side that took over that area in my body and the pain went away.

This clairvoyant example was not showing me a crystal clear visual of what was to come or a vision of the past. Sometimes the messages you get through your clair channels need some deciphering or decoding. You might have to do a little detective work to discover what your Spirit team is relaying to you. This is specifically with clairvoyance, since the clairvoyant images may come through as symbols or signs. With claircognizance, you would immediately know what the message was, and with clairaudience, you would hear spirit telling you.

CLAIRSENTIENCE

Clairsentience means "clear feeling". It is feeling the answers, messages and guidance from Heaven. Do you ever have a gut feeling or a hunch about something specific about to happen? You advise someone accordingly about it only to discover that it later ends up coming true. Do you get a strong feeling of joy that you or someone else is on the right path and this ends up coming true as well? Do you get a fear of dread when walking into a room that someone is not of a high integrity and that turns out to be true?

These are examples of having strong clairsentience. It is similar to being an empath, but the difference is that an empath has sympathy for those around them while a clairsentient will *feel* the guidance and messages relayed to them. An empath is likely to be able to develop their clairsentience quite easily if they choose, because half of the ingredients are already there. Earth Angels are a group aligned with having the gift of clairsentience as well. They are generally sensitive and intuitive more than any other. Earth Angels will sacrifice themselves for the well-being of another, but if you are an assertive Earth Angel, you no longer accept any form of abuse or hostile environments to be in. This is why your higher self leaves those situations. Earth Angels are incredibly strong even if they or others may not be privy to this.

I have a good degree of clairsentients. Having

two to three dominate clairs is rare, but I might have gladly handed the clairsentients back. It can be draining always feeling and sensing everything and everyone around you. For me, this was not always a good thing, because I sensed all of the bad and pending dooms too. I could not stand being so sensitive that when I was old enough I began drinking and later turned to drugs and other addictions. I reached for anything that would dull and turn it off for good. My clairsentients was so highly calibrated that it bounced off the Richter scale once the violence in my childhood kicked in. I found there was nothing positive about sensing every feeling that existed. It took me a good part of my life to see it as a gift.

You know you have clairsentients if you feel and sense every little thing around you. You are not just feeling and sensing it, but these feelings are giving you a sense of what is going to happen in the future. You can work on having all four primary clair channels opened regardless of having two dominant clairs.

Chapter Three

EMPATHY AND
EMOTIONAL DETACHMENT

If you rely on your hunches and intuition when receiving accurate information, then you are feeling the answers. Not all communication is in a form you would recognize such as a voice *(clairaudience)* or in front of you like a vision *(clairvoyance)*. Some of it is through your body by feeling the guidance *(clairsentience)*. Trust these gut feelings, as they could be the answered prayer you've been hoping for. Focusing on the stillness within you is where the real truth and answers are. There are a great many souls who feel every little bit of nuances around them. They may not necessarily sense the future as a clairsentient would, but they are feeling and absorbing everyone's energy. Those people are called Empaths. As an empath myself, I used to self-medicate with anything and everything possible to turn it off. This included drugs, alcohol and pills. You name it and I likely did it. That didn't go over quite well as you can imagine. There are pluses to knowing what someone is going through just by having them walk past you or stand next to you. You are the one that everyone feels comfortable going to when they want to dump their problems off of themselves. This is why it is absolutely vital you take care of yourself and run your life like a strict executive. Do not be afraid to say, "No, I cannot help or listen to you right now." Because you feel other's energies and sympathize you will have to work on being assertive in saying no without guilt. You need to take care of you first, before you can help someone else. As an empath, you might immediately know whether or not you can possibly help someone or if you should avoid them altogether. You soak up all of that energy including the horrible stuff.

I have to shield every day before I go outside. This is by asking Archangel Michael to surround me with a permeable white light of protection. I also had to train myself to control the flow of emotional information that people outwardly direct without realizing it. If you are sensing fear, which is a common empath trait, then mentally call out to Archangel Michael to come in and extract those fears from your body. As an empath, you are more prone to absorb negativity and/or addictions. When this happens you can invite in entities you cannot see that feed off of you. You may suddenly feel drained or reach for that addiction again. This is why as an empath you need to take excellent care of your body and your surroundings more than any other might. Treat yourself delicately and with kid gloves.

Being an empath can make it impossible to be in crowds unless without choice like a concert for example. I typically avoid places where I know it'll be taxing on my soul energetically. Standing in a grocery store line can make you susceptible to soaking up the tampering energies easily. Oblivious or innocent human souls will stand too close to you in line and the empath will absorb that person's energy. Those psychically in tune tend to have trouble with being in crowds because of this. This is because they pick up on all of those frequencies around them. Someone who is oblivious is not very much in tune or aware. Your soul is so large that it doesn't fit in your body. The light of the soul is six feet all around your human body. Someone is going to be standing in your light. If they are a negative human soul, you will latch onto their toxins while it attaches itself to you. When you arrive back home, you feel drained and crave the need for a nap and do not know why. If a stranger is standing too close to me in a grocery store line or a friend is harboring negativity, then I can feel my energy being lowered. This is an example of someone who is soaked in stress or any other negative emotion. They are called *energy feeders* because that is what they are essentially doing. They drain you of your sensitive energy leaving you worn out or agitated.

If you live in a fast-paced busy city you might notice that people mostly tend to go to the store because they have to. They feel it is a drag and as an empath you can feel all of that. They stop by the store on the way home from work when their stress level is in peak form. They may be at a job they do not like or one that is cutthroat. They take that energy out into the streets and bump into other human souls who pick it up and then pass it around to someone else and so forth.

I am currently in Los Angeles and it is busy everywhere no matter what time of day it is. Unless it is in the middle of the night, the streets are always packed. It will likely take thirty minutes to travel when it should typically take ten minutes. You are also sitting in dirty smog breathing that in along with the fumes of other people's cars. The roads were not built to handle the volume of people and cars that exist today. This only adds more stress onto everyone's shoulders even if they do not realize it. Many people pass out of this life early due to the long term effects of this stress. There are things I have to do to push the energy away such as shielding.

As an empath, you have to be careful that you do not absorb other people's energy or spend an immense amount of time worrying about them. You will need to train yourself to observe *emotional detachment.* If you have been in the military or you have had to live at the hands of someone who has abused you, then you likely had developed a good level of emotional detachment. If you are faced with hostile energies you might react negatively in some way. You might lash out or feel completely drained. You can work on emotional detachment by breathing in deeply and exhaling until you have calmed down and relaxed. Train your mind to take these incidents that come at you objectively. Also avoid stimulants and heavy amounts of caffeine when possible as that exasperates your nervous system prompting you to be more volatile. See the innocence and naivety in how someone else might be behaving. Showcasing emotional detachment might make you seem cold or aloof to someone. Pay no mind to any of that and do not feel guilty about it. As an empath, reaching for that place of non-guilt is where emotional detachment lives. If you are the go to person where everyone comes to you with their issues regularly, then it is essential for you to practice this emotional detachment.

If you ruminate wondering how to make the world and the people in it more compassionate, aware, and humane towards one another, then you will need to learn that these are opportunities for you to practice emotional detachment. It doesn't mean you don't care, but everyone is living out their own karma and learning their own lessons. It is not your job to learn those lessons or fix any of that for them. What you can do is BE loving and supportive, but emotionally detached enough that their stuff doesn't get to you and affect your life in a negative way.

Emotional detachment doesn't necessarily mean that you don't allow yourself to feel anything. It means that you separate your emotions from your thinking and take the broader view of a situation to assess it without feeling it. Emotional detachment takes practice, and it's more of a learned skill than an intuitive one.

I went through periods of guilt, because although I have my own neurosis I had finally reached a place in my thirties where I was doing well spiritually, emotionally, physically and financially. I have been taken care of in all ways since then as I paid my former Karmic debts to society. I ultimately surrendered permanently to the care of the Spirit and the Creator. I eventually became a spiritual teacher and warrior living in the Light as best as I possibly can. My team showed me that I lived a tough life and came out of it unscathed. I did not back down from going after what I wanted to do. I would take on everybody else's issues as the go to person. The angels had said that would darken and drain my energy if I did not back down. It was important to take constant breaks of "me-time" to re-charge. If I didn't take my time seriously, then I would grow scattered and sloppy in my connections and choices subsequently experiencing burn out. I reached a point in my life where I had acquired enough knowledge and experience with people to understand what makes them tick. My writing turned me into a master observer and this is all emotional detachment in action.

Chapter Four

MUSINGS ABOUT CONNECTING
WITH THE SPIRIT WORLD

The next dimension, the spiritual plane that is right after this one, the place your soul travels to when you're done with this Earth class is closer than you think. Many believe it to be far, far, away and unreachable, if it even exists as some might say. It absolutely exists even if some Earthly souls are unable to fathom it. Some have lost hope or faith due to their life choices and circumstances. This causes them to express doubt. The next spiritual plane where most departed souls move to is three feet above the earth plane. This is why many gifted Mediums and Psychics successfully communicate messages from others in the spirit world so effortlessly. This is due to the spirit world being right above this plane running parallel three feet away. Keep in mind that the Earth plane is huge rising high above the clouds and into the ethers of what you know as "space" where the planets orbit. The first etheric plane above this one runs parallel above that. Actually "they" consider us and them as all one plane. I separate them to indicate that it is an entirely different world. There are other dimensions beyond the immediate etheric plane after this one where most souls move to next.

There are many gifted Mediums who communicate with the other side professionally. However, it is important to remember that you are also a gifted Medium whether you use your abilities or not. Like any muscle in your body, you need to work it and use it often. The more weights you lift at the gym with your body, the stronger your body becomes. The psychic muscle is the same concept.

When you have a psychic read, the future is always probable. What is seen coming up in your life can be altered significantly if you act on free will. For example, if you choose to deny the soul mate that is in your path repeatedly or you choose not to take a particular job, etc. This will alter your path and a new path is formed. For example, if you were meant to be in a long term soul mate relationship with someone, but the other person denied it and left, then they did so out of free will. Your spirit team will work with this soul mates team to bring you both together again. If this is unsuccessful, due to this person denying Heavenly guidance and acting out on free will, then your Spirit team will work to bring you a higher soul mate more aligned with you.

We all have varying ways of communicating with the other side. Some may be more open to seeing other souls that have departed, while others can feel them. You have those, such as myself, who hear them, as well as those who know they are present without questioning it. I have been hearing them for as long as I can remember. Some people use divination tools for confirmation of the messages they receive from the other side. Calling someone up with your telephone is similar to a divination tool. Spirit can deliver messages to you in a variety of ways, such as through your senses, through signs, symbols, and numbers or through the use of a divination tool such as an Angel Board, Tarot or Oracle deck. The tools are used to communicate or confirm what the reader is picking up on from the other side.

It can be painfully depressing to see some human souls unaware or confused and unsure of what is going on around them outside of the material world. Much of the hesitance some human souls have with crossing over is the fear of the light and that judgment or eternal Hell is associated with it. This is due to teachings during their upbringing on Earth. It is hammered into their psyches by those around them and adopted as second nature.

Your ego remains as is when you cross over. No longer stuck inside your human body, you carry the traits you had while living an Earthly life. This includes any negative traits or thought patterns. If you let go and move with the process of crossing over, you will notice any pain you were previously carrying being lifted off your soul effortlessly.

Those who pass onto the other side will at times visit their loved ones on Earth to make sure they are okay. Your departed loved ones are doing fantastic, but they know that you may not be or that you may not understand their death. My Spirit team has informed me that many of the departed souls tend to assist one or more of their grandchildren if they have any. Their own children are older than their grandchildren. Because they are older, they are likely set in their ways and do not need much guidance the way a younger person might.

It is okay if you do not know who to call when addressing an angel or guide. Simply calling out to Heaven will bring the right guide, angel or spirit who specializes in your specific case. You can request a Heavenly soul to assist you with something particular. Results are not always instant. You may have a soul on the other side working with you for several months. They will stay with you for however long it takes to fulfill what your request is. The spirit guide leaves when their assignment with you is complete. They move on to help other human souls requesting assistance. They often have their hands full when it comes to working with human souls, because they are dealing with souls who enjoy operating from ego or using free will, which can affect and alter their circumstances significantly.

When you struggle to receive Heavenly communication, then you block it from reaching you. The ethereal communication cord is much like a telephone wire to the other side. This dims considerably when there are blocks around you. Relax and let go of the need to receive a Heavenly message and allow it to flow into you naturally.

When you shift into a greater and more fulfilling spiritual life, you need to watch what you ingest into your body. You need to be mindful of what and whom you allow to hang around your vicinity. Your sensitivity is growing and can only absorb so much before it needs to recharge. It can no longer handle that much psychic input in one sitting. I had to make some strict lifestyle changes when my portal had cracked open again after having been bathed in addictions. There was a distinct difference in my connections when I was clear minded as opposed to being heavily intoxicated, high or after having consumed bad foods.

When you stop and detach from whatever emotional or stressful issue you are experiencing, then you are apt to receiving the answer needed from your Spirit team. When you are under stress or worry, then that blocks the communication lines with Heavenly helpers. Ask that your Spirit team remove and lift the stress and worry off your body so that you are more receptive to the answers and messages they are relaying to you.

Your first response as to who is communicating with you is the right answer.

Second-guessing the information you receive pushes you further away from your initial hit of who or what it is. You will know who it is without a doubt in the world. Trust what you receive.

There is no greater feeling of freedom than connecting with Spirit. You can do this anywhere, but in a nature setting or calm atmosphere, will allow the connection to be clearer. This allows Spirit to lift the weight of your burdens off your soul. You realize that nothing else matters. Human egos force restrictions upon other human souls and have no basis in reality. The forces come from ones lower self and are typically born out of fear.

When guided, I often deliver messages I receive through Spirit to others, but then I walk away from it. All I do is act as the messenger in those cases. It is up to the person on the receiving end to decide how they wish to proceed or act with this information delivered. Never volunteer the information unless you are certain your Spirit team insists it will benefit someone in a positive way. Never divulge where you are getting the accurate messages from to a skeptic. When you are a messenger of God and Spirit, you must take great responsibility in the way you relay those messages.

All human souls have psychic abilities. "Psychic" is not reserved for the John Edwards' or Sylvia Browne's out there. Famous and well-known psychic mediums are where they are at because they have chosen to devote their lives to this work. They have turned it into a winning career. The same concept applies to how you are at your own job. When you have been with a company or doing a certain type of work for a long period of time, then you get better at it. You can almost do it blindfolded. This is essentially how successful psychics have turned what they do into a lucrative profession. No human soul is more special than anybody else. Everyone has diverse gifts with varying ranges within the realm of psychic abilities. It is all a matter of tuning in to discover what your specific gifts are and then re-developing that muscle. One works out their physical body this same way. You need to work your psychic muscle out as well. When you were born, your soul was 100% psychic, but you were also given the dreadful ego in order to test you. The ego creates roadblocks and barriers in all aspects of your life. You also learned negative behavior patterns from those around you. Those learned traits connect you to the material and superficial world. This is only some of a handful of things that can prevent someone from being in tune to spirit.

The ego is not a part of you to punish you, even though it seems to do a good job of it at times. Its intention is to challenge you. You must learn from your challenges. When you learn, then you grow. Growing your soul is in order to know what is right from wrong.

Since all human souls have egos this makes it difficult for the majority to believe or comprehend that they indeed are psychic. The word psychic has a negative connotation to it if one is a skeptic. They may not realize that they are picking up messages from their own Spirit Guide and Guardian Angel regularly. Everyone has at least one Spirit Guide and one Guardian Angel who is with them around the clock, from birth until death. They offer guidance along your path while answering some of your prayers on divine timing. If you are not listening or following this guidance, it can make your journey on Earth a bit bumpy.

You receive messages from beyond almost effortlessly when you are relaxed, stress free and happy. You also receive messages and guidance when you are tired. I have talked about how I successfully conducted a particular Mediumship session with a girl's departed loved one on the other side. I did this while running on no sleep. When you are in a fatigued state, then you are too tired to let your ego get in the way. It is fascinating that the human ego has incredible power that it can block someone from receiving messages from the other side.

A good place to start is by thinking back to particular circumstances where you might have professed something that later came true. You remember how that information came to you naturally from seemingly out of nowhere. Notice the way you came to this information and if it was the same process each time. This will give you a good direction on where your specific psychic abilities lie.

You are not alone and have at least one Guardian Angel and one Spirit Guide that works with you on the other side. Yet, you become absolved in your own neurosis and problems attempting to do it all on your own without accessing them. Many souls run into roadblocks or

frustrations over something they are try
happen. I have to stop them and say
asked for help?"

They will protest, "Oh you're rig
about that."

I will get a message from them later. "I asked
like you said and it worked! Wow!" They will
describe the outcome of what happened after days
of no movement. They asked for help and suddenly
the answer they needed appeared.

You have to give your Spirit team permission
to help you and intervene in your life. Let them
know you want them to work with you. If you do
not, they will sit their idly watching you wiggle
around in stress and annoyance. Do not just ask
them for help, but then let it go and let them get to
work on it. When you let go, the resolution comes
to you much more quickly.

There is one way you can tell the difference
between heavenly guidance and your lower self or
ego. When you receive messages from heavenly
spirits, you will never experience fear, anxiety or
dread. The messages they relay are full of love, even
if they are warning you of something negative.
There is still a sense of peace or an uplifting feeling
that all is okay.

Sometimes I receive clairvoyant visions
especially while experiencing a lucid dream
sequence. This was the case where my Spirit team
delivered a message to me when I was in a deep
sleep. In this instance, they were showing me what
many around the world were going through at that
particular time. In the dream, they are taking me

...to what might appear to be a nightmare to the average person. I can handle most anything and I am used to some of the abrupt ways delivered messages reach me.

I walked into my house and a man was standing there. Naturally, as you might do, I wondered why he was in my house. He approached me and asked me for money. Without thinking twice I said, "Sure." I reached into my pocket, but then he quickly moved towards me in an uncomfortable way. I asked, "What are you doing?" Before anything else could happen, he pulled out a blade and stabbed me in the heart with force. I felt a huge sharp pain as if it was really happening and I was dying. The piercing of the stab in my heart was pulling me deeper into the other world. My eyes shot open and I realized it was no longer happening. I collected myself and then brushed it off knowing it was a divine message. I knew they would reveal additional information to the stabbing image when I would fall back asleep again for part two.

I fell into another deep sleep not long afterwards to allow my Spirit team to give me the rest of the message. I heard a loud banging like construction echo going on for minutes before it stopped. I wandered through the house in the dark at 3:00 am. I was wide-awake and noticed the tiling from some of the walls were broken and crumbled all over the floor. I could see the pipes within the walls. I saw pieces of the plaster on the floor in other rooms too. I glazed over it confused and perplexed. Mind you, it was happening as if it were real time. There was no comprehension that it was a dream. My eyes shot open and I looked around noticing everything was fine. No tiling or plaster on the floor. I knew then that it never happened.

I did not have to ask my team for more clarification because I understood their language and message. They filtered the messages through my crown chakra. The stabbing in my heart was telling me that it was to deliver the message that many around the world are experiencing heartbreaks in breakups of all kinds. This was backed up by the abundant amount of messages from readers I was receiving. They were all experiencing a hard relationship break up at the same time. The deterioration and crumbling of the walls in my home in the darkness were telling me that these breakups were significantly painful and happening out of nowhere. The darkness is the heavy grieving felt. Those who were experiencing these break ups and endings were feeling as if their whole world was crumbling down. The structure and stability they had come to understand was falling apart. There was much heartbreak within the dynamic of many of the connections. This was no surprise to me because at the time we were in the midst of the Venus Retrograde transit. This causes relationships of all kinds to break apart abruptly or the connections are strained.

When you experience the kind of heartbreak where you cannot find the will to pull yourself back up, call on heavenly assistance. Archangel Raphael can help bring feelings of peace and serenity.

Archangel Azrael can help make the pain and transition out of a bad relationship much easier than without heavenly assistance. Archangel Raquel can help restore balance within you and your partner, friend, or whoever you experienced an abrupt issue or ending with. Know that you are not alone or ignored. It may not seem like it when you are going through heartbreak, but it is happening for a reason that will become apparent at the right time.

The Archangels are powerful, benevolent beings who can show up for anyone who asks. They are unlimited after all. Archangel Michael is with me on a daily basis and always shows up even when I do not specifically request him. This is because I made a pact with him a long time ago that he would be my protector on my journey here. In another incident, I was in a deep sleep and within another vivid dream as if it was happening in real time. There was a nasty dark ugly poltergeist throwing things at me and around me. Poltergeist or noisy ghosts exist. They are not as bad as Hollywood horror films like to portray. These spirits do not realize what they are doing. They are stuck in a limbo atmosphere, which is similar to the Earth plane, but no place for any roaming soul. This poltergeist in the dream was intense due to its real nature and by infiltrating itself into my dream. My heart fell into my stomach and I ran out of breathe. I shouted in the dream, "Archangel Michael!" A huge boom sound rang out loudly like a native drum. My surroundings lit up with super bright light. My eyes shot open as I caught my breath. An overwhelming feeling of love took over my soul.

Some have lucid or vivid dreams which evaporate upon wakening. Sometimes this is due to the use of drugs and alcohol. The effects of drugs and alcohol interrupt ones sleep cycle and diminish the amount of REM (dream state) input. This can cause you to forget your dreams upon waking. When you release the need to consume drugs and alcohol, your body will go through an automatic detox. The detox process is not always smooth as inner stuff is coming out of you. When you are no longer on negative substances, your dreams become more lucid. Your consciousness travels out of your body during your dream state. Often times when going through withdrawals or detoxing, even months after the elimination, can lead you to experience fear in your dreams. Your subconscious mind and your lower self are in a tug of war while in the sleep state.

Use of alcohol and drugs hinder the brain chemicals that transmit messages. When you no longer consume heavy amounts of negative substances, then your brain's neurotransmitters go through a process of re-alignment. Part of this causes an out of body experience. Some will experience flying dreams as well as dream situations surrounding fear. Your soul is not grounded in the physical world. This can assist you in delving deeper into working with methodologies of healing and working with your clairvoyance. Remembering your dreams and having repetitive out of body experiences are signs that your third eye and clairvoyance have opened or are in the process of opening.

As a sensitive vibrational being, you will sense things more than the average person would. You enter a store where everyone else seems okay with the energy, yet your Spirit team gives you a warning sign to leave the store. You feel it in your gut area and perhaps your heart rate accelerates. You might hear your Spirit team calmly ask you to leave the store. They ask you to purchase your items somewhere else. Some of these warnings might happen while in a metaphysical store as a reader named Karen explained to me. She believed that because psychics practice there that it must be okay. Unfortunately, that is not always the case. Someone within the store may operate heavily on ego or they are unable to reel the ego in. This can attract in negativity into these stores. Perhaps a hostile client wandered into the store that day and their energy was so intense that it stayed in the store long after they left. You will know if it's not safe if you walk into the store and suddenly you experience negative thoughts or mood.

Everyone has the ability to connect and communicate with a spirit guide or angel. Some see it, others hear it, some feel it, while others know it. Pay attention to your senses as they are communication channels with the other side.

Have it set in your mind that they communicate with you every day. The more you practice, remain aware and in tune to your senses, the easier it gets to work with them. You are always communicating with them, even if you may not realize the messages you are picking up on are indeed your Spirit team.

Sometimes someone might experience a specific health scare or near death condition that re-opens the portal to Spirit. Those situations crack it open for good. I talk about how this process happened for me in my book, *"Reaching for the Warrior Within"*. My connections have been ongoing since I was coherent, but there was a health scare in particular that cracked it wide open again. It was the turning point for me as I shifted into a higher consciousness. There was no going back to my previous life and I would not have had it any other way. Archangel Michael visibly appeared as the introduction to what the next chapter and beyond would be.

It is not always up to the angels or Heaven to do it all for you. It is up to you. When will you take action? When you take action, then Heaven meets you more than half way. They will not hand anything to a human soul who sits around doing nothing, but waiting and complaining on when life will hand them something great. Heaven waits patiently for this soul to see the blessings they have around them. They watch this soul put in the work required before they intervene.

Chapter Five

Karmic Debt

Every decision and choice you make daily, whether good or bad, has a consequence. As this energy is put out into the universe, you have set in motion what is to come to you in the following year. The life you're living now is a direct result of the actions you previously made often without realizing it. This action or thought energy is multiplied to the third power and beyond. This means that what is mirrored and directed back to you due to one small misguided deceptive action, decision, or thought, ends up being something that pulls you and your life down. Do the right thing and learn to make sound choices in your life. The Karmic energy associated with things such as thieving and deception is huge. Understand the repercussions that will come out of an unreliable choice in the end.

In the field of spirituality, there is the teaching of giving away your gifts with nothing in return analogy. However, there needs to be an exchange of energy. There have been some who protest why psychic readers charge for their reads. The psychic reader is working and performing a job. They have bills to pay in this current modern day age, but there is the exchange of energy factor as well. You're giving someone goods in exchange for goods. This is a balanced energy. You find other avenues and ways to give freely at the same time without monetary payment.

The human souls who have incarnated from the Realm of the Wise One are a little odd walking to the beat of their individual drum. They do not typically fall into any of the boxes that one might associate someone who is spiritual to be. There are varying levels and different degrees in so many areas within the context and area of the spirituality genre. There's room for all of it in what everyone is contributing from within it. Part of the *Warrior of Light* meaning is that you will have to go to battle at times in correcting what needs to be righted. This is what my Spirit team has been instilling in me since human birth. With that come some issues naturally. It invites in unwanted antagonism and energies. It's nothing that a warrior cannot handle or ignore. They have a job to do and anything outside of that is noise.

A woman named Beverly had told me a story

of how her Guides and Angels wanted her to get involved with a soul mate to work on karma from a past life. Beverly said that she understood the lesson meant to learn already. She did not feel the need to go through with the relationship. She explained that her Guides and Angels insisted this soul mate is her life partner and that she is contracted to help this soul mate in this lifetime.

My Spirit team immediately flagged a couple of spots with this inquiry. One of them is that your Guides and Angels will not insist that you connect with a soul mate you do not want. When it is your true life partner, there will rarely be any long term resistance or doubt. Any doubts entertained come from the ego which wants to sabotage you in taking any responsibility in improving a soul mate connection. If your guides and angels ask you to work on karma with a soul mate, then trust your guidance. Regardless if you see the lesson clearly, you agreed to work this out with this person before you entered a human life. If you do not, then you'll have to do it in a later lifetime. It will not evaporate, disappear and go away.

If the connection is abusive in some form, then that would be a reason to step away. Your Spirit team would not insist that you remain in a hostile situation. This is your ego talking as it revels in seeing you suffer. Working on your karma with a soul mate can include coming to a place of forgiveness for any slights this person or you have done to the other. If there are negative feelings you have within you about this person, then that will be applied to your karmic thread that needs to be resolved. It can also be that this particular soul mate needs to balance out karma with you. By you agreeing to the connection, you're allowing this person to have that opportunity to bring peaceful closure to your union. Peaceful closure is where you are both content and at peace with wrapping the relationship up.

When souls cross over, not all of them share the same space. Your soul travels over to the dimension and area your vibration is at. Only on Earth do you share the same space. Criminals or rulers such as Hitler and Hussein do not get a free pass in Heaven. They have to go through a rigorous review as they're crossing over. The laborious reviews occur en route through what is called the back gate. You are made to know what you had done to every single soul that you harmed. Imagine going through the feelings and thoughts of one soul you harmed. You are experiencing what that one soul went through at your hands. Now add the array of an infinite number of souls that were harmed by your hand. This is a grueling process to go through for human souls such as Hitler. You have to pay the karmic debt back, which results in more than one repeated lifetime. These are Earth lifetimes where you are put in situations that are less than stellar compared to your previous lives.

It is not difficult to see what one would incarnate back into a human life as. For example: An abusive, racist, white, slave owner in past history would incarnate for another Earth lifetime as an African American. This is in order to balance out that soul's Karma with the hopes or intention they would unite all races together since we are all one. The separation that exists is designed and ordered by human ego. It has nothing to do with the real reality in the spirit world. Someone might have distaste for homosexuals. In a past life they assaulted and caused harm to anyone considered to be homosexual. They stirred up the masses with hate words about them. This has its own karmic retribution. What do you think they incarnate back into another life as? A homosexual. God will teach you to walk in another man's shoes by putting you in those shoes if it'll get your soul to experience compassion. Of course this doesn't necessarily mean that if someone came into this life as an African American or as a homosexual that it is due to karmic debt they owe their soul. These are merely examples of the possible ways it could go and has gone for some souls.

All soul's have much work to do while here. There are things you're working on within you. Perfection isn't demanded by Heaven. The anxiety of perfection comes from your ego. Heaven wants you to put in an effort and do the best you can, but to be kind and compassionate to yourself and others at the same time.

About 75% of human souls will do a repeat life. This is at least one repeat life, which will be less than the current one due to that souls' Karmic debt being so great. For example, Katherine is currently living a life that is well to do with money and abundance consistently flowing in, and yet she is horrible towards other people on a daily basis.

She has built up karma due to being cruel to others around her. She will be asked to do a repeat life whereby the money she has in this life will be taken away. In the next life, she may live in squalor and poverty in a third world country. This is why it's important to do the work now and become as a great a person as you can be now. Examine your life with a fine tooth comb. Give yourself the critique you find yourself giving to others. Catch yourself when you are destroying someone else's life in the many harmful measure of ways that exist. Be aware of everything that is happening outside of your physical body and your material needs. Be mindful when you are walking out on someone in a soul mate connection who is good to you.

Karmic debt is not resorted to the criminals of society. Even good souls build up karmic debt. It's almost impossible not to build up karmic debt because you're having relationships with other souls that have complicated emotions tied to it. This is where soul mates come in. You might have a tempestuous love relationship with someone where it ends badly. Years have flown by and you still have not forgiven this person. This is displayed in how you continue to speak ill of them or scoff when their name is brought up. In this case, you have built up karma. The karmic debt is not that you reincarnate in a horrible circumstance necessarily, but you typically reincarnate with that person repeatedly, one lifetime after another, until you are on even keel with their soul. Reincarnating on Earth is the choice of both souls.

Reincarnation is the belief that when your soul

exits your body it immediately reincarnates into another lifetime. There is a time period that goes by before you reincarnate. You have the choice to do so or not. The newer Earth souls do reincarnate more than once. One Earth class isn't enough especially if that soul did not evolve or gain crucial knowledge in the first lifetime. There is a difference between reincarnation and incarnation. Reincarnation is the soul re-surfacing in a new Earthly life to balance out previous karmic debt. They will learn additional lessons that were not gained on the previous round. Whereas incarnation are the souls *choosing* to incarnate in order to contribute something positive towards humanity and the planet.

There is much talk and fascination about reincarnation and past lives in many circles. My Spirit team has said that knowing ones past life is not important. It's fun to know for entertainment purposes and out of curiosity, but most of the time it's withheld from your memory bank because it's considered unimportant. What matters is your current life. You have worries, stresses and concerns throughout your life. Can you imagine if you had these same worries about circumstances that happened to you in another life? This is why it's withheld from your memory bank.

What would it be like if you recalled all of your past lives? You're upset and someone asks what you're upset about. You say, "Oh something I did in the 14th century still plagues my thoughts."

The only importance knowing your past life has is that it helps you heal major ongoing issues you're carrying and battling with in this lifetime. If you're someone who has spent their entire life focused on lack, then there can be a connection between that and a past life of yours. If you're always having love issues or you have trouble forgiving others, then there can be a connection that exists in one of your past lives pertained to that. This isn't to be confused with ones current upbringing where fear may have been instilled in you in this lifetime at the hands of someone else. It may have nothing to do with a past life. As it stands human souls love to conjure up fear energy. Just log onto the internet and read the headlines of the latest news and gossip stories. The darkness of the ego is prevalent on every street corner.

Chapter Six

Heaven's Gate

In the ancient book it talks about how people lived for hundreds of years during the beginning of Earth's conception. To get into a book that is popular and controversial in a measure of ways would prove exhausting. I can only relay messages that my own Spirit team passes through me and not what human society says or follows. There are some altered truths and some fictionalized accounts within the book due to the perception of society during that time in history. If it is clear at how easily led humankind is today, then it is understandable how even less evolved they were hundreds of years ago. Look at how the masses follow one another like cattle today. Notice how they rally together in lynch mobs to crucify others they disapprove of. This is evident in the media and in the comment boards online alone. Behavioral instincts are predictable in the way others follow one another. This is apparent in how human souls treat each other, which is often in every way, but kindness. Look at how they are on the playground growing up as children in grade school. See how some of them are within the confines of their own households. If this is the case today, then you can imagine what humankind was like centuries ago when a book like the Bible was being put together.

Back in historical times, human souls were more in tune to all things beyond. They spent a great amount of time outdoors in nature and amidst the fresh air. They did not have phones, cars, computers and all of the other electromagnet technological gadgets that prevent others from truly spending time with one another today. Being able to connect to someone today so quickly has its grand advantages, but what about the disadvantages? The radiation that exists in all of these devices and appliances is contributing to rapid health declines. Technological communication gadgets have caused decay in face to face connections that used to be long lasting. When you grow up in a world that trains you to receive gratification instantly, then you're going to experience some issues.

Anything having to do with fear, guilt, or low self esteem in the great book is mythology. Only a human ego would write something like that, especially during a superstitious patriarchal society. Women were not considered equal until far into the 20th Century.

Some of the truths are that people did live longer than they do today. How the Bible or historians have come to the rough estimated numbers on how long people were living would deem unfeasible considering that the Calendar had yet to be invented or perfected back then. Despite this, I have been shown that humankind did live longer than we are now. This is easy to grasp considering that humankind had not yet turned the planet into the ticking time bomb that it is today. The stresses that are placed upon humankind now have become largely unreal and too complicated to understand. These are stresses that did not exist at the beginning of time. They did not have mortgages and rents. Humankind has turned their needs into complications. They have created this mess and others are here to attempt to reverse and correct it.

When life was simpler centuries ago, humankind was outdoors in the fresh air and that air was breathable. They'd wake up as the sun rose every morning and head out into nature for the day. They were not confined to boxes all day long. This is the way they do now in cold lifeless offices with poor unhealthy lighting. Imagine the toll that will take on you. Envision the repercussions on your health and physical body after a couple of decades.

When human souls leave their office at the end of the day, they race home in a box that is their car only to walk into another box, which is their home! The amount of time that humankind actually spends outdoors is limited compared to how it was centuries ago. You might race outside for a quick walk only to retreat back inside immediately. The diets and foods were not yet contaminated, processed, and pumped with every toxic chemical you can imagine. In the beginning of Earth's time, human souls were not consuming hot dogs, chips, and ice cream on a daily basis. It's likely not surprising that in the beginning of time humankind lived a lot longer.

Some human souls are placed in the back seat when they pass onto the next world. They are on hold in Heaven above. They do not go through the front gate where you are greeted by angels, but through the "back gate". These are the souls who were careless or inhumane. It's the place you move to in order to learn about forgiving yourself for harm you have caused others. It is where you make amends and choose to work on your soul to be a better person in the next life. This can take some time to come to fruition. Others who lived in the Light on Earth and contributed positively towards humanity grow small light wings.

The back gate is another tunnel of light that is more or less taking the long way around into Heaven. This route is typically reserved for those who caused a good chunk of damage to other people while on Earth. They have quite a bit to amend, review, and come to terms with. The length of this path depends on how much needs to be reviewed with that soul. This is to also prep them for the work that lies ahead in the spirit world. This process also includes restoring their soul beyond the human part of their ego which is still with them.

You are having an Earthly life to elevate your consciousness by opening up all of your senses which enables you to be a conduit of the light. Be aware of what's going on around you, but remain detached from any drama. Do your best to be in tune to your soul's higher self. Focus on the source of love that resides inside you. This light of fire and spark dims due to the influences that human souls are assaulted with regularly. This light never truly dies and is always accessible at the hands of your higher self. Avoid becoming lost in the fog that finding the light within you is difficult to locate. It exists and resides permanently within you. Crank up the volume of this light and allow it to wash over you in a baptism.

Your personal team of Guides and Angels know more about what's coming for you, than you do. They don't always share or reveal this because there are experiences you need to be enlightened about on your own. This is why they insist that you learn to trust them and know that all will be well in the end. They know that what might be currently going on in your life is for good reason. Nothing lasts forever, so patience must be practiced. Have fortitude and understanding that there is a plan. On the flip side, some effort on your part must be put in as well depending on what the circumstance is. For example, if someone is complaining they do not have any money and yet they're sitting around at home surfing the internet instead of being diligent about looking for work, well what do you think will transpire out of that? Your Guides and Angels meet you half way when you show that you are doing what you can to assist as well.

Human souls have destroyed and wreaked unforgivable havoc on Earth for centuries. They continue to function in chaos at an accelerated rate. Throwing Children into a room full of toys will inevitably bring on tantrums and power struggles. This ensues as the child's ego attempts to dominate and nab the toy of their choice before anybody else does. This is animalistic and often seen as innocent by the parent or guardian's ego of that child. Heaven knew this would be the case at the conception of Earth. A place was needed where new souls would go. It was known that it would be much like throwing Children into a school playground in hopes they all get along.

There is great optimism in giving human souls the benefit of the doubt that they will carry this love they are born out of through the duration of their life. It is intended that the human ego will not drift too far astray. It is understood that catastrophe would be and is possible. Angel soldiers and souls on the other side stand in line to be born into a human body. They are the human souls contributing goodness for the betterment of humanity.

Earth is a place God created where souls are sent for the purposes of learning, teaching, growth or to have a first life run as a human soul. The ones on Earth for the first time tend to have the most amount of ego. They are naïve and innocent in their actions through the eyes of the angels, but they will not get away with harming others for free. A debt must be paid back from their actions. This will be collected at some point for that particular soul. They are the ones that harm, hurt and hate with no care in the world.

Chapter Seven

RECEIVING MESSAGES
FROM HEAVEN

When you grow spiritually and transform into a warrior of light, you will find the messages from Heaven cracked wide open. At times I use the information I receive from Spirit and incorporate them into whatever I'm working on. I have always received messages from my Spirit team asking me to step in and assist particular people. I tend to volunteer the information without always telling that person where I'm getting my answers. Some might get uncomfortable when they know the source. Only when I know they are open to it do I reveal where it came from or how I know something that has helped them. To connect to your Guides and Angels it's important to breathe. Take a deep breathe in, hold it for a few seconds, and exhale out any negativity. Continue to do so until you are deeply relaxed. This can take anywhere from five to fifteen minutes or longer if needed. There is no set time frame as every individual has their own process. The point is that you are completely relaxed and stress free. You might be under stress and not realize that you are.

The messages from Spirit reside throughout the elements of your breathing. This is one of the reasons it is important to exercise regularly because that increases oxygen that is fed into all of the cells in your body. Those cells are all telecommunication receptors with your Spirit team. Those same cells close up when you are causing damage to them through things like poor lifestyle choices, diet, addictions and negative emotional states such as anger, stress, or depression. Head into nature whenever you can to soothe and center your mind and mood. I have found the communication with my Spirit team to be clearer in those instances. I am always active and on the go. I do not sit still or relax easily unless I'm writing. For me to be able to reach an immediate calming state to connect even deeper means that anyone can if they put in a little bit of effort. You do not have to sit Indian style in the grass by a tree. You can stroll through a park or hike into the mountains breathing all of that wonderful nature in.

Do not allow your nasty ego to pull you under

and obsess over triviality. When it takes over, you fixate over what you don't have or what you feel is lacking in your life. You panic with impatience over circumstances that are not taking off quick enough. You grow upset that no one understands you and you feel disconnected from others. God and your Spirit team understand you and that is all that matters. Take a step back and be of service and gratitude instead. The angels and your guides are perfectly content and blissful. Many of them including those that have crossed over become of service in some way and that brings in good vibes to everybody involved. To get to that space, close your eyes, take a few deep breaths until you are super relaxed, and mentally or out loud ask, *"How may I serve?"* Allow whatever positive impressions you receive to be the answer. This can come to you through any of your clair communication senses such as seeing, hearing, knowing or feeling.

TRUST IN DIVINE COMMUNICATION

It took me a long time to trust anything. There were times I did not trust my own abilities. My Guides and Angels point blank said something terrifically beneficial that applies to all of us: *"We want you to know that the messages you're receiving are not your imagination. You are discounting your own abilities by continuing to question your reception of input given specifically to you by us, often to help others. We ask you to stop doubting and trust more so that you can make better use of the input you get and not question it so much."*

A solid way for you to track your own interactions with your Guides and Angels is to keep a journal of the information you are receiving. Even if you think it might be your imagination write it down anyway. Keep this journal for one month. Record each message you believe you have received, whether you believe it's from your Spirit team or your own intuition. After a month, go back to it and jot down the outcome of that message. You will be able to tell the difference between the self-generated messages and the messages received from your guides. Trust the messages you receive and do not doubt it. If you make a mistake or you end up being wrong about something, big deal, keep on going. Your ego gets in the way and creates unnecessary negative self-talk that is not based in truth. Sometimes you make a mistake, but with practice you improve at focusing on what is your higher self and what is not. Anyone can connect to the other side who works at it. You have to take care of yourself on all levels, such as physically, spiritually, mentally and emotionally. When you have raised your vibration on those key well-being traits, then the closer you are to receiving accurate, mind-blowing, heavenly communication.

Everyone connects to the other side in various ways. For me as a clairaudient it can sometimes be like tuning into a station on the radio. I can hear the static in my left ear as I'm tuning in and moving the dial until I hear my Spirit team clearly. This is how I heard about the 2012 United States Election trajectory and outcome over a year prior. With all of the noise in the world, I tuned that out and heard the real voices of Heaven break it down for me. They listed each of the running candidates that were dropping out of the race in order. They told me who would be the United States President in 2012, which later proved to be accurate. My mind then drifted off wondering what an incredible place this would be if politicians and its people were all in tune to their own Guides and Angels.

People get so caught up and obsess in the meaningless drama in and around their lives that it bewilders Heaven. You just want to slap them away from that place. Some of the tougher spirits on the other side absolutely do that for you. It's a waste of time engaging in pettiness instead of focusing on high vibration activities. Gossip, arguing and negativity are the biggest time wasting culprits of all. There are people who live in that state around the clock. It contributes absolutely nothing beneficial to anyone especially yourself. The energy is toxic. Clairvoyantly it appears like a dark, old attic filled with mud. There are stringy webs, cords and insects crawling all over this attic. This energy within that person festers and grows like mold. It is a big contributor to common diseases such as Cancer, Hypertension, Diabetes and much more. This is why you must take care of yourself in all ways and take the body you have with great earnest.

EXAMPLE OF SPIRIT INTERVENTION

One night I felt extreme thirst, which was odd considering I had just finished drinking a huge tank of water. I eyed my bottle of water, but then something prompted me to crave juice, which rarely ever happens. I buy juice and it sits there. I went into the kitchen and opened the fridge door eyeing the juice selection I had. I heard a hissing noise as I was pulling the juice out and poured it into a cup. I put the juice container back in the fridge and heard the hissing noise again. I opened the fridge and peered in confused looking at the light bulb. "Is that where it's coming from?" I closed the refrigerator door and was startled at the stove on my left. The stove burner was still on! I quickly turned it off, "Oh my god, I'm gassing the place up full of carbon monoxide!"

Had I not received a sudden craving for juice, I would not have gone back into the kitchen until the next morning. It would have been another twelve hours later to find the stove still on or an explosion. Who knows what would've happened. The thirst *(also known as clairgustance)* and sudden crave for juice was prompted by my Spirit team. I was nudged to head into the kitchen in order to catch this. This may appear so insignificant and slight that someone's ego may discredit it calling it pure luck. When you are fully aware and in tune you start noticing all of the little synchronicities and signs that are put in your path at the right time to help you. You do not notice these signs when you are oblivious or absorbed in your ego. The way your Spirit team guides you is also through these seemingly insignificant situations.

RECEIVING MESSAGES THROUGH MULTIPLE CLAIRS

I was on the phone reading for an inquiry. I breathed in and out mentally asking to receive messages on him. Purple forms and shapes came at me. Seeing purple is common when your Third Eye Chakra is open.

I said, "I am shown a red car and a guy with brown hair driving it."

He said, "What kind of car?"

Hearing the word through my clairaudience channel I said, "Ford."

I continued on describing the clairvoyant pictures I was seeing. "The weather is sunny out, but it's cold. People are rushing around in heavy coats. There are tall buildings around and it looks like a big city. There is a subway or trolley rushing by above ground."

He said, "I think you're talking about my brother. He has brown hair. He just bought a red Ford Focus and he's in Chicago right now. They have a train that is above ground."

Hearing the word through my clairaudience again I said, "Who is Michael?"

He said, "That's my brother. He's the one you saw with the car."

I said, "I don't know why they showed me him when I mentally asked about you."

Then through my claircognizance and sense of knowing channel I said, "Okay, he's moving or wants to move."

My friend said, "Yeah, he's in Chicago, but has mentioned moving to San Diego. I don't know how serious he is about that."

There are times when just enough information is revealed, but you are not always shown the entire picture. One of the reasons is that your Guides and Angels will not live your life for you. They may offer suggestions, but then it is up to you to figure out what is the best course of action. If you make a mistake, then they will help you out of it if you ask them to intervene. Your life will brighten in beautiful ways when you invite your Spirit team into your house.

It is not necessarily fun when you know the person you're in a relationship with is straying. When I was twenty-nine years old, I was in a relationship with someone who was not faithful. My guides showed me the one I was with in a moving vision along with a dark figure in the background. They told me there was someone else in the picture with us. Two weeks later I discovered it was true and I left the relationship.

A friend of mine called me to talk about someone he just started dating. He gloated at how this guy made him feel. His voice trailed off as he spoke. I took a deep breath and closed my eyes. I mentally said to my Spirit team, "Show me this guy he's talking about." I saw a guy with dark hair flash in front of me. I interrupted my friend and said, "This guy you're talking to has dark hair."

He says, "Yeah, it's black, so Kevin, then he…" He continues on not realizing I'm in a different space.

I saw the flash of a tattoo on this guy. "He has a tattoo on his arm and looks like on his back too."

My friend is quiet and low. "Yeah. He has one on his arm and it wraps down his side and onto his back. Wait a minute. How do you know this? Never mind. I know how."

You have access to Divine information about others when you are in tune to the vibrations within and around you. Breathe, relax and connect with the other side. You'll be amazed at the messages you receive.

HEARING THE RIGHT VOICES

There are times where you might not know if it is your imagination or your Spirit team. When I was a child I would sometimes wonder who was talking to me. I grew to understand that I'm super hard on myself, so that's how I am able to tell the difference between what's me and what is a higher being communicating with me. Your Guides and Angels do not give you a hard time. You give yourself the hard time. This is your ego and how you differentiate. Your ego wants to make you uncomfortable and insists that you are incapable of doing anything.

Spirit starts sentences with, *you* or *we*, while you or your lower self and ego start sentences with, *I*.

For example: "**I'm** not going to take that art class because they will all discover **I** am not creative." Whereas the angels will say, "**You** will take this art class as **you** are going to be a successful painter. Pay attention when we communicate with you as we have important guidance on the next step once you complete this action."

Knowing that you are not alone and there are Spiritual Helpers on the other side assisting you to have a peaceful life full of abundance takes practice, faith and trust. I have off days as we all do, but I'm fully aware of those days. I pray to release the burdens that I accumulate as it comes. I have battled trying to connect with so much going on in my mind that it's impossible to shut it off. There was a time in my earlier life where I worried whether or not I was on the right path just like anybody else. I would be working on writing pieces where I'm blocked and experiencing a blank slate, then when I'm knee deep in it I would wonder if I was making a mistake. You can see how the lower self wants to argue with your true higher self and delay you from doing anything.

Chapter Eight

IGNORING HEAVENLY MESSAGES

Sometimes reading for others or intervening to help someone does not always go beautifully. There are times where I've read for others in the past, or relayed messages randomly to someone, yet they refused or denied the guidance and messages. This ultimately ended up created in a downward spiral effect as explained in the next story with Lisa.

My Guides and Angels asked me to let Lisa know that she needs to get outside more. This could be a calming locale such as a park surrounded with trees and flowers to awaken her state of mind pulling her out of isolation. They said she needed to open her windows and let fresh air into her place daily. She also needed to exercise more than she currently was. This much needed advice was blocking her and preventing her from reaching a higher happiness with work and love.

Her response was she "can't" leave her house and doesn't have time to add in an extra day of exercise. She informed me that she is unable to open up her windows as they are purposely boarded up. She was upset with the messages I relayed. I was shown that she would remain stagnant indefinitely unless these simple steps of progress were made. I did my part, which was to deliver the messages. How someone chooses to respond to them is not my business. I deliver the messages or guidance and then I walk away. In the end, it was discovered that four years after this read, she was in the exact same place she was when the messages were originally given. No movement in career or love had been made. When you shun Heaven's guidance, then you're not shown the next step. This can take years if you choose to ignore the original message.

Your Guides and Angels relay messages that will take you from Point A to Point B. Sometimes these messages are not what you want to hear. They may advise you to stop drinking alcohol as it prevents you from pursuing a successful career. Your ego will not see the two going hand in hand. Heaven knows exactly what you need to do to get to the place you are dreaming of. Paying attention to the guidance of your Spirit team will help you reach greater heights. If they are asking you to get outdoors or clean up your diet, trust it is for good reason.

When you refuse or opt out of following the messages and guidance of your Guides and Angels, then you essentially choose a path of continued misery with no hope for a breakthrough. The wisdom from Heaven may at times seem outlandish or impossible to follow at the time it is given, but it is important not to discredit it. They are doing this for your benefit by assisting you with making major life changes so that you can achieve a higher happiness and be at peace. Ask them for help if you are feeling fear and afraid to leave your home. Archangel Michael is the Archangel who helps with fear. Ask your Spirit team for help in finding a better doctor if needed. Archangel Raphael can assist with this too. They will not throw you to the wolves unarmed. They know the direction your life will take once you start taking active steps to improve your situation. Life is not always easy and there are and will be turmoil and troubles that enter your vicinity from time to time. There are other times where your decisions or lack of making a decision brings you unwanted chaos. When you have your Spirit team working with you, then the roadblocks that pop up will be more manageable, than they would be if you hadn't invited them into your life.

You remain in relationships longer than you should have only to discover you were with someone who was using you for superficial reasons. You spend fifteen years living with someone only to run into one argument after another. Neither of you seek the assistance to stop the cycle or end it, so it endures causing strife and heartache.

You have two people in love, who are drawn to one another and should be together, but both live in fear that if they take that leap in joining together that it might end badly or they'll get hurt. Avoid self-fulfilling prophecies and know that you have the power to manifest whatever it is you want. There are countless books written about this. They all talk about the same thing. The reason they all talk about it and write books about it is because it is true. It does not matter if it is a holy, spiritual, or philosophical book because the content is all similar. It has been proven that someone with a positive mindset ends up achieving and fulfilling all of their dreams. Those same people that received miracles due to constant optimism can all attest to this.

Someone who is buried in negativity will struggle against the choppy current growing weaker by the day. In order to evolve and grow your light spiritually, you must seek to improve yourself and become a healthier person by making sound choices. Those who refuse heavenly guidance end up stuck in the mud. If someone's ego is too big, then they don't want to hear how they can improve themselves. They are under the delusion that there is never any need for improvement. There is always room to progress, as that is what growth is. As a Wise One from the other side, I have a larger ego than more sensitive earth angel souls. However, my ego is not the kind of ego that deludes me into believing I do not need to grow and change. I'm an ever evolving work in progress.

When you go through a rough time, retrace your steps and examine how you arrived at that place. You create and manifest your future with the decisions that you make today. If you acted naively or blindly in a previous love relationship, then you welcome in the potential hidden deceit that hits you later. This is what some call Karmic retribution. If you do not notice the red flags, then you will bear witness to the outcome that leads you to a negative place at a later date. When you are in this state it could feel as if you will never get out of it. You are in a place with immense possibility and freedom to carve out a life on your own terms. You do not want to allow yourself to be hindered deeply in the past. Marinating in anger, stress, or any other negative emotion blocks you from moving forward. You have likely known or heard of someone who is in that state around the clock. This person may be in that circumstance for decades over one incident where they felt crimes were done on their psyches. Do not allow that to stop you from finding peace and love within and around yourself. I had a rough tumultuous life growing up. I did not allow that to prevent me from seeking happiness and going after the things I wanted and getting them.

TAKING RESPONSIBILITY

Life on Earth moves super fast in this modern day world. It is overcrowded and spilling out over the edges. Everyone needs to pull their own weight and contribute something towards humanity in a positive way. For many, seeking out a partner in life whom you love is beneficial. This is so that you can share the journey with an immediate companion and share the expenses. You have the soul fulfilling through the means of a soul mate companionship, and you have the practical self taken care of all at the same time.

Back in the late 1940's and 1950's, America in particular had crafted out a neatly organized plan where a man married a woman and went off to work to provide for her, their family, and their home. The women stayed home to keep house, clean, cook, and raise the kids. It wasn't long before women noticed this imbalance. They had a burning desire to contribute something beyond keeping house as well. America had a real taste of it when World War II happened. The men went to war while the some of the women took on the jobs that men would typically do. It's now essential that couples share the responsibilities, regardless of the genders involved within the love relationship. Living expenses and survival modes continue to rise, while work pay stays relatively the same. We're all somehow supposed to accept this greed mentality of taking from others while making them pay a higher price to receive the basic necessities of life.

Stephanie stopped working after she married her second husband, Matthew. There was no reason for her to stop working and I only saw danger up ahead when she did. The job market and the economy were going to weaken in the early 2000's as I was shown. If one of you within the duo loses their job and is unable to find another one, you're going to have more problems than you are prepared for. You can see how making unwise decisions in the past can lead you to where you are today. There is a cause and effect to the decisions that you make on a daily basis. Everything can always be corrected once you are aware of how you played a part in it. See the steps you need to take to improve and do it.

The immediate reaction of anything negative that's happened to you comes from the ego. This is where it quickly goes into blaming someone else for leading you to where you are. There is a profound saying that says being a victim is not your fault, but staying one is. Pull yourself up by your bootstraps and get to work at empowering you.

Stephanie's reasons for not looking for a job would be things like: *I'm too old. No one is going to hire anyone who is fat. I don't have a degree.* The ego makes one excuse after another to stop you from doing anything. People of all ages, looks, and those who do not have a High School Diploma go out there and find fulfilling jobs because they have something else: Drive, persistence and passion. They are self-taught and believe in themselves. Let your true-self shine through every interview and endeavor you undertake. The majority of the jobs I obtained had nothing to do with anything except my personality, passion and drive. I walked in unqualified and untrained for each position. I would become friends with the employer during the interview. They would be connected to someone with a personality rather than just another face answering the same job preliminary questions. I'd take over the meeting and would wind up obtaining the position over someone who had more experience or a college degree. In fact, I recall one employer who said he was meeting other candidates who had the fancy experience and degree after our meeting. Yet he added, "…but between you and me, I'm going to be hiring you. I still have to meet them out of courtesy." He did hire me as they all did. Communicate with your Spirit team and ask for their assistance with you when job hunting. I've mentioned this to some who discredit it. They do not ask for help and therefore do not get it. The world is changing rapidly and many are paralyzed with fear and anxiety about the future. The angels can guide you through these changes and give you solid guidance that you can trust. They help you stay calm during crises and heal away negative situations, while extracting the lessons contained therein as well.

SPIRIT IN THE SKY

One morning I awoke and immediately went into a channel with my Guides and Angels. This is common for me as I always find it to be a great way to start the day. You are super relaxed and open to communicate. I have heard from some that the second they open their eyes they have worry on their mind. This is no way to set the tone for your day and I've been guilty of it too in the past. Give your worries to Heaven in a mental prayer or affirmation in the morning. Start your day right. Whenever you are stressed or tired, then that is your body trying to tell you something. The angels urge you to pause and retreat as much as possible so that you can see the answer. They know when your soul is over stimulated and when you cannot afford to absorb any more input from the outer world. The energy of the outer world is intense everyday now, which is why it's crucial to take several time outs. On days that you are unable to, please do your best to sense, feel, hear or know the voice of your higher-self coming through the noise. Even if you're unsure if you're making contact, know that you are. They are always responding even if you're temporarily blocked and not in the mind space to receive.

This one particular morning when I awoke, they asked me to turn the radio on. I reached over and hit the "on" switch near my bed.

The first few chords of the next classic rock song began called, "Spirit in the Sky". I thought that was incredibly fitting and pretty humorous. Those in Heaven have great laughter and senses of humor. This is why they urge you to have the same. They prepared me for the day and to remember that we're never alone. They prompted me to get a move on. Your Guides and Angels around you communicate to you in various ways and sometimes through music! This was their way of telling me they enjoyed connecting if only briefly after I woke up.

Have faith, trust and open your heart to Heaven and your Spirit team. Pay attention to the repetitive signs and symbols around you, as they can be the answer you've been looking for. Remain detached and connected to your inner voice as much as possible on a daily basis. It doesn't matter if you're mentally checking out at times when you have practical priorities to attend to. You will still get those done by keeping one foot on the ground and the other in the spirit world. You're advised to take pause, relax and contemplate often. In this process, you're clearing out all the old energy accumulated in and around you, which can be draining on your overall being. Your soul needs constant rest amongst the demands of Earthly life, therefore it is always okay to take regular time outs and not feel guilty about it.

Chapter Nine

REACHING FOR THE WARRIOR WITHIN

I have lived several lifetimes in one having grown up open to a wider variety of experiences than most people can handle. And many cannot handle some of the things I have partaken in. I discuss my rise from the ashes to becoming a Warrior of Light in my book, *Reaching for the Warrior Within*. I grew up in an abusive household. This led my personality to fragment and split off into many different "selves". I was smoking cigarettes from age fifteen to twenty-five.

I started drinking alcohol heavily before I was seventeen. By the time I was the legal drinking age of twenty-one, I was already a full-blown partying alcoholic. This then led me to heavy drug use from getting stoned daily with marijuana to cocaine and Methamphetamine use. I was involved with drug dealers and those in escort services in relationships when I was in my late teens and early twenties. I was in one dysfunctional relationship after another where they all strayed at some point in the end. They were searching and dating around or were bathed in their own nasty addictions. They were committed one week, then non-committal and confused the next.

Sometimes you have to get beat up a bit to get a little street smart. Once you've been in the darkness, then you can easily help others navigate out of it. I dissolved or reduced my addictions with the help of my Guides and Angels. A complete turnaround was made when I was twenty-six years old. Before that, I was putting in energy to obtain toxic vices. I was soon putting that energy into more healthful ways of living. My connections to the other side opened up again in miraculous ways when I went clean. Since I was a teenager, I was guided by my team to study nutrition and more health conscious ways of living. This was regardless that I was abusing drugs and alcohol. I've been exercising regularly since I was a teenager, but in my early 20's my darker side and the lower self was running the bigger part of the show. The situation would entail me doing a line of cocaine and then chasing it with a glass of carrot juice. I lived in immeasurable degrees of good and bad, light and dark, walking that fine line into both elements equally.

My earlier life was about survival and living in fear. I ran for shelter in a plethora of toxic poisonous addictions instead. They were harmful to my body, my psyche and well-being. There was always one bad circumstance after another going wrong. I gradually and quickly began to discover early on in my life that I was happier and more successful not partaking in those previous poor ways of living, but it took some time to get there. My Spirit team was always with me backing me up. They helped me obtain all of the jobs I ever wanted, including getting into the entertainment business and getting in front of the right people. It was like hitting many forks in the road that included a different choice.

I was clearly shown each choice down each road. One road was full of rocks and thorns surrounded by drugs, alcohol and other toxic addictions including people. The other road was lit up with a bright light and a timeline of positive events headed out into the distance for me to see. It was clear to me which road I should head down on. I was an intelligent young man, but breathing in constant pain. Despite hopping from the light road to the dark road sporadically, I knew I did not want to blow it. I knew what they were handing me and I needed to receive it in the right spirit. This would be by responding positively to these Heavenly gifts. Doing so would ensure I am taken care of in all ways. This ended up proving true. I have always been communicating with a team of Guides and Angels on the other side. We all have this ability, but for me it was as natural and fluid as you call a friend up on the phone. The communication with them was dimmed to a good degree as a teenager when I rebelled against authority and swam in a sea of addictions. With the constant assistance and guidance of my Spirit team, I cleaned up my act and made a commitment to Heaven.

Although the demons live buried in me, I have quieted and tamed them for some time. Today I live comfortably and happily in the Light. I love me more now than I did growing up and into my twenties. My whole life has been a series of phases that has led to the joy that I experience now. I haven't wasted one-minute in my life always changing, forever evolving, gaining knowledge and life experience beyond someone who has lived 100 Earth years.

The biggest phase was when I made this official spiritual transformation as described in my book, *Reaching for the Warrior Within*. It was a pivotal transition, almost like a graduation in a sense. My world became brighter, but there were significant life choices I had to make to get to that place. This was not done alone as my Guides and Angels have always been communicating with me and guiding me down the path I needed to be on. I left one juncture of my life that was full of intolerable circumstances and entered blissfully into the next one with immense excitement.

I can listen to other people's stories, trials and

tribulations without judgment and follow it with my input, which includes the wisdom, inspiration or healing words that Heaven has taught me over the years. Even while buried in my own addictions, my Spirit team filtered the answers and guidance through me. I had blocked much of their instructions out from being high, drunk, full of anxiety or depressed. Addictions and negative feelings of any kind cause a block between yourself and your Spirit team. They are always communicating with you and nudging you along your path of course, but you are not in a state to receive their communication. You are ignoring them without realizing it. This is until you get a smack in the back of the head to take notice of the danger you have been putting yourself in.

My work and communications with my Spirit team of Guides and Angels grew to be daily during my official spiritual transformation. Before that, it was randomly and whenever without effort. Then I made a commitment to invite God and my Spirit team into my life permanently. They were instrumental in working with me to remove anything that was holding me back. They assisted me in adopting a new improved lifestyle and way of doing things.

Because the changing that was taking place was on the extreme side to something better, this would mean that I could no longer be around certain people. This was similar to when I quit drugs in my early twenties. Even though I had stopped doing drugs, I still hung out at the homes of these drug dealers, hustlers, ex-cons and users. It was about two months after I stopped the drugs that I cut them all out as well. Not only could I no longer relate to them sober, but their energy was lost in the darkness and self-destruction. I was quickly moving onto a brighter path and had to eliminate it and them, or my foot would always be on the wrong side of the road. I never questioned it. It was as if I was standing in front of an open golden door feeling excitement and anticipation. I turned around to see the drug users one last time in their disintegrating dark hell environment. I smiled and waved goodbye. There were truly greener pastures, a rainbow, and a pot of gold shining at the end of that yellow brick road I headed down instead. That was more attractive than the previous life I was living. There would be no way I could deny it.

Chapter Ten

RANDOM MESSAGES FROM SPIRIT

Guides and Angels do not always divulge ALL information on what's to come for each individual. Some of the reasons are that you need to have certain life lessons and experiences on your own before you are shown the next great step. You need to be content with where you are at before the good stuff comes in. Some souls can take years before they get comfortable with that if at all. Come to the realization that it is best to be grateful for what you have now. Complaining or being upset about it doesn't do you, your body, or soul any good. I've witnessed others live in that perpetual state of unhappiness indefinitely wondering why no miracle has come about. The odds are that these mini-miracles have been brought to them, but they were too over-involved in despondence to notice. I've certainly been there myself, but I've noticed that the moments where I am completely content and not fixated on the future, then the great career position comes about or the next love relationship enters my life.

HALLOWEEN

Halloween is one of the more popular holidays celebrated on October 31st. Nowadays it is mostly a time where people have fun with it by dressing up in costume, watching scary movies or visiting haunted houses and theme parks. There are myths and legends associated with the holiday, but most of it is not true according to my Spirit team. It is a day to remember the deceased. It ended up taking on an entirely new meaning over time. People started to associate the dead with ghosts and goblins. You can see how the holiday can easily take on a life of its own.

When I asked my Spirit team if the veil is thin between our world and their world, I received a surprising, 'yes'. The reason is mostly due to there being so much energy focused on the dead by human souls around Halloween time. Because this energy is so potent on the day of Halloween itself, this invites and attracts more of that energy in from the other side. Even though people are doing it just for play, it is having an effect. The effects are harmless to an extent, although you should shield your soul on Halloween or October 31st. Take precautions that you do not invite unwanted negative spirits into your vicinity who drain your energy. Those on the other side are pure, but there are spirits who are what some might describe as being in limbo. These souls refused to enter the light sometimes due to fear of what might exist such as judgment, etc. Instead, they attach themselves to human souls. They are usually attracted to darker lights and people bathed in addictions or in negativity in some manner. They coax that soul to continue on with the addiction or negativity.

The period around Halloween is actually a time of "transition" and "abundance". This is right on par with being about mid-way through the Fall or Autumn harvest in the Northern Hemisphere. My Spirit team did not get into the whole Halloween thing, but focused on using the Halloween energy to manifest abundance. Sow the seeds of what you want in your mind. It is a very powerful time including on All Saints' Day which falls right after Halloween on November 1st, as well as the Day of the Dead, which runs from October 31st through November 2nd typically.

THE EGO'S WRATH

The ego is what convinces you that you are not qualified. It delays you from moving forward with your life purpose. It prompts you to experience any negative emotions such as jealousy, stress, sadness or hatred. The ego is your lower self, which is not of God. It is the part of you, which acts childish and immature or causes drama. Frustrated and fearful human souls might join in a gang or cult. It covers up what they feel is lacking with a false confidence. It is also a learned trait. A human soul does not enter this life desiring to enter into a cult or gang. When you think for yourself, you do not have any interest in latching onto others to form a gang or group. Do not allow your ego or anyone else's for that matter to convince you that you are not qualified or not ready for something. You were born ready and qualified. Ignore the negative voices that attempt to sabotage you. Go after what you want and do not allow doubt or reservation to enter the equation

Human souls must live with one another and learn how to love. You learn how to love when you accept that others are not like you. They do not live the way you do. Outsiders who have different interests and lifestyle choices than you will enter your vicinity. Your vicinity is your community, city, workplace, or on any level. Do you welcome them with open arms or are you immediately suspicious? Accepting someone with love is having an understanding that different people live in this world with varying belief systems and this is okay. This does not mean you must accept and love someone who is harmful, gossipy, and violent towards others. Accept and love those who have a different way of living than you without judgment. This includes those who have varying religious or political beliefs. This also includes those who are of a different nationality or sexual orientation than yours. If someone is acting out from their ego with these types of circumstances, then pray for them and walk away. I realize this can be easier said than done, but I'm sure you've noticed when you have been equally judgmental towards them that you've experienced an uncomfortable feeling inside.

A greed mentality exists in every part of the globe. One example would be the kind that plagues America. One of the biggest shopping days of the year in the United States is called "Black Friday". This takes place the day after the Thanksgiving holiday every November. It is a day when material items are marked down to a great degree. It is only a handful of products which are marked down for a specific time limit. They are mostly products you do not really need. This leaves many fighting over material items. If you do an internet search on the crimes and violence broken out on Black Friday, you would be amazed. Thanksgiving is a holiday that has more or less forced most of America to head to their family's house to break bread and cook a turkey. The meaning of the long weekend has lost its flavor. It's now all about shopping. It's about Black Friday and now Black Thursday. More retail stores are opening in the late evening on Thanksgiving Day. This is of course a backwards step for humanity, where human priorities are dominated by greed. Close up shop. Take a break. Chill out and relax!

This is anyone and everyone that is participating in Black Friday on Thanksgiving. The exception is the employees who are expected to work.

I've always found Thanksgiving to be an odd holiday. This is especially when you dive into the history of how the holiday started to begin with. Human ego started a war on another culture of people in order to take over the land. On the flipside, I'll accept a holiday that does its best to bring people together. This is the point of Thanksgiving in current modern times. There will never be enough of bringing people together going on. What is unfortunate is that a holiday needs to happen in order for this to be accomplished. This should be all year round.

When I connected to my Spirit team for messages for Thanksgiving and Black Friday weekend, surprisingly the first thing that came up was LOVE. Love is the biggest feeling experienced when you cross over. It is Heaven and the spirit world's mantra. Love. Joy is right up there with love. Remember what is ultimately important to your soul and why you are here. It is to love. It is to give and to spread love. This mantra should be adopted everyday and every minute of your life. When all else fails, remember: LOVE. Think and breathe the word always. Be grateful. Be thankful and above all....love. When that fails, love again, and repeat.

One of the strengths that everyone has in common is the capacity to operate purely from a place of love. Everyone was born with this gift. Negativity, stress, emotional instabilities are all learned traits. Love is what you are made of and what you were born with. It is the only place you can find true power and strength.

Anyone can connect to Spirit who works at it. You have to take care of yourself on all levels, such as physically, spiritually, mentally and emotionally. When you have raised your vibration on those key well-being traits, then the closer you are to receiving accurate, mind-blowing, heavenly communication.

We are all on the precipice of a new energy. Heaven has sent millions of souls to enter this world to usher in this change and set the example in a myriad of ways. The spirit world has been sending souls to enter into human form throughout history to enact particular changes that progress God's Earth. These same human souls were crucified. They were people from Jesus Christ to those who were accused of witchcraft. They are and were those who had views that were out of this world. The new group of what some refer to as Light workers, Indigos, Crystals, Rainbows and many others has increased with great magnitude after the 1960's. More of them were rushed in through the 1970's and even more into the 1980's, 1990's and beyond.

SHIELDING

Because of the harsh energies plaguing the world in other people, it is important to shield yourself and your soul. Shielding is the act of calling in your Guide or Angel and asking them to shield you with protective white light. If I happen to run into someone with a bad mood, I call in Archangel Michael immediately and ask him to shield me from their energy, while extricating them from my vicinity as well. In the past, I would've let the person's mood affect me or I would take responsibility for their upset. Those days eventually became long over to the point where I was a completely different person then.

Be careful not to over shield either yourself or your business. Sometimes you might surround yourself with so much protective light that you are invisible. No one can see you or your business. Ask that the light heaven sends down to shield you be permeable. This means that only the love enters the shield.

If you do not have deep clairvoyance, then you might not see all of the lights that are around you and every living thing, person, organism or plant. The lights can be seen from Heaven, but not necessarily for the average human soul who tends to block that connection and ability. The exception is someone with a strong clairvoyance channel.

Shield yourself when reading media stories. Most of it is toxic drama that the media puts in front of the masses on a minute-by-minute basis anyway. The planet is enveloped in a thick tar of dark debris that lowers vibrations and causes a massive array of health issues in the process. Be aware of what is going on in the world to an extent, but do not get buried underneath all of it.

It does seem to be in your face whenever you turn your head. When I'm not in front of the computer, I'm in the dark to what's going on in the world. This is of course unless a friend mentions something major going on that I had not heard of. I do not watch television, but when you log into your email account for example the headline ticker is splattered all over it. It might be on your friends social networking wall thread when you log into that. The great thing about my official social media group account is that I can choose what high vibrational accounts I like or follow, so all I see on my wall are those posts. On my personal social media account for example, they are filled with friends or acquaintances who sometimes post things that are more gossip, negative or toxic worthy. I skim over it quickly, although it is rare with my bunch to begin with, but it's still there at times. Using your social networking account to vent or express negative feelings on a regular basis sends this energy to others and back onto yourself.

I shut that down years ago and do not hang around it. Those who know me personally know my deal and how I operate. It is rare that I see drama brought up with me. It does happen once in awhile, but others can sense I am not interested as I have a good measure of apathy and detachment. I might say something along the lines of helping someone, and then continue on my way, rather than assisting in pro-longing the drama. I am in and out, and away quickly in those situations.

I am outside and in the car and travelling through highly tense areas with wall-to-wall cars. You have stressed out drivers on the edge. This is where one can be most affected because you cannot escape it, unless you move to a quiet country and nature like setting with little to no people. This is why it is important to shield before you hit the road. This is so that you are not absorbing all of that wasted energy darted in your direction. When you absorb this energy it weighs you down, jars with your emotional state, and makes you feel tired and irritable. A friend once suggested smiling and waving to tense drivers or people walking by. Notice their face warm up and relax. Kill them with love and kindness! Put in an extra effort to spread love.

CORD CUTTING

Whenever you come into contact with a friend, family member or love relationship, you form a cord to them. This cord looks much like a gasoline hose to a clairvoyant. The hose is hooked onto you and this other person. If the person you have a cord attached to is moody, angry or showcasing other negative emotions, then this will harden the cord and cause you to absorb that energy from them. If a loved one has crossed over to the other side, your cords are still connected. This is the case if you had a strong tie on Earth. These are energetic cords and both departed spirits and human souls share this same energy. Cord attachments are not always negative, but they can be. You would know if the cord has turned dirty. You feel weighted down or lethargic when you think of that person. You feel negative thoughts or anxiety when that person is on your mind. This means you need to cut the cords with that person, especially if it is preventing you from functioning or moving forward.

Cord cutting is where an angel or spirit being cuts the etheric cords of attachment that form on your soul. Archangel Michael is the go to Archangel for cutting cords. There is no difference whether the person is on the Earth plane or in the spirit world. It is an etheric cord connecting two souls. Your soul can have hundreds of cords attached to it, as there is no limit. However, it is unlikely one would have that many at one particular time, because you would feel it and know it. Your mind is not thinking of hundreds of people at once. If someone has not been on your radar for some time, meaning you have had no communication for years, then it is not likely you would have a cord attached to that person.

These cords attached to someone else can be communication devices with that person. This is why married or committed couples for example know and sense what is going on with their partner without them uttering a word. The same goes for exes. Yes, I have communicated with exes telepathically on occasion in the past. This was long before I controlled my thoughts. This communicating with them telepathically prompted them to reach out to me, which depending on the ex is not always a good thing. Call on Archangel Michael to cut those cords daily. I go into more detail about Shielding and Cord Cutting in my book, *"Raising Your Vibration."*

RAINBOWS

The Rainbow colors are a mixture of colors that different hierarchy spirits exude and radiate. They are high vibrational colors and lights. Archangel Raziel shows up wherever rainbows or rainbow colors are. There is nothing negative or cryptic about a rainbow connection. They are reflections of light created as a message from Heaven. They are one way that someone on the other side is sending you a message if you are seeing the same symbol repeatedly. Heaven will communicate through repeated symbols and signs that have the same pattern. It would depend on what type of help you are asking for if any to decode those symbols.

If your question or request for Heavenly assistance were in regards to a work promotion or something having to do with material success, the rainbow would be a sign that the pot of gold is coming up or good news. The rainbow can also be a bridge or a passage that things are looking up. It also means hope and assurance that God is indeed present. Of course whenever God is present it is always a reminder that you need to be exuding love more often. He is always present, but when He is showing signs of His bigger presence, then it would show up in many forms including rainbows. He does not reveal his presence through violent acts despite what some might believe. Those are the acts of human ego. God is all love.

Chapter Eleven

PSYCHIC INSIGHTS

Heaven and the Spirit World have an aerial of view of the trajectory of your life. They tell me that if human souls could see what they could see up ahead for them, they wouldn't be complaining and whining so much. Every human soul can see what's up ahead for themselves. Someone had mentioned they did not believe in psychic abilities, but they believed that people were intuitive. Psychic or intuitive is the same thing. It does not matter what you call it. You're tuning into your core senses, which are communication receptors with worlds beyond this one. All souls have this ability to read better for themselves than anyone else can. Accurately reading for yourself or anyone is impossible when your ego is ruling the show that is your life.

How often have you received an internal jolt that something in particular was about to happen, and then it did? Even the non-believers can take a step away and recall those incidents where the psychic phenomena did indeed occur for them. You can do this by raising your vibration and tuning into what's outside of physical distractions. Trust the repeated messages you receive. No one can do that for you better than you can. Have patience and faith that what you desire will work out in your favor in the end. Sometimes it's not what you predicted or what you hoped, but you learn to realize that in the end, how it turns out is much better than you had envisioned. There is a reason you're living the particular life you are at this time.

Heavenly guidance sifts into your consciousness almost effortlessly while in a dreamlike meditative state. When you wake up from sleeping at night, it's almost immediately that you have forgotten your dream, even though you awoke from it minutes ago. This is what it's like before you enter an Earthly human life. Before you enter this life, your memory slate is wiped clean except for hints that include your life purpose. This is similar to your memory being wiped clean when you awaken from a profound dream. Only hints of this dream you had while sleeping are left if at all.

You made a contract with your Spirit team

before you entered a human life. In this contract are things like the soul mates you would encounter, the things you would endure, your life purpose, when you will pass on and head back home. This is similar to the dream state when you're sleeping. Your memory is fully restored when you cross back over and head home into the next plane.

Some live an entire Earthly life and do not fulfill their contract completely. They may not come to this realization until the final days on their death bed as a human soul. They realize they are indeed going to leave their physical body. The reality and the fear might hit them at that point. They might say, "Why didn't I forgive him or her?" or "Why didn't I allow love in from this person?" These words filter through your consciousness as you transition home to where you came from in the spirit world. Your Spirit team on the other side greets you along with Archangel Jeremiel. They go over your entire Earthly life. This consists of things such as what you did and what you didn't do. What you did to others and what others did to you. What you accomplished or neglected and so forth.

I receive some pretty common psychic related questions. The first common question is about love. Readers write me frustrated about not being in a love relationship. My Spirit team says that the desperate need to have a lover is what blocks one from obtaining a lover. It's the negative feelings associated with that need which includes a fear that it won't happen. This goes back to the saying: "Let go, let God." When you let go of the negative desire and panic to obtain a lover, then the lover shows up. I can attest for me personally that this is true. Every serious love relationship I have been involved in throughout my entire life to date came to me and developed when I wasn't looking for anything. I was in a state of perfect contentment before it happened, and then it happened naturally.

The second common question is surrounding one's career. Others are trying to figure out what type of career they want, or what job they should go after, and in what industry. The response my Spirit team gives me on that is to think about what your passion is beyond making money and then you have your answer. The desire to chase money as ones sole purpose will leave you dejected. I can also attest that the response to this question was accurate for me. I have never gone after a job or career position for the purpose of monetary gain. I went after it because I had a passion and desire for that type of work or position. The money wasn't on my radar. It ended up flowing in naturally and in great abundance more than expected. The increased financial flow for each work position I accepted in my life was the icing on the cake.

Pay attention to your senses when deciphering the incoming Heavenly guidance while on your life's journey. The guidance could even come in the guises of déjà vu moments. Déjà vu moments can be psychic hits of the future or of the past. The past can be a previous life or someone else's past. This can be the case even though the déjà vu moment is playing out as if you're the main character.

The future is what's to come. This also means

not necessarily a vision of what's coming for you personally, but it can be someone around you. The way dreams and clairvoyant images come to you are not always direct. It may show you a particular vision, but one that is not necessarily going to play out exactly in the manner it's being displayed. Clairvoyant hits sometimes need to be decoded and interpreted.

The ego desires things now. I'm impatient myself regardless of knowing what's coming up ahead at times. Part of working on spiritual evolvement is learning the nature of patience and tempering the ego. Sometimes another person's guides will communicate with mine. My guides will then interpret what the other person's guides are relaying. They communicate at a fast pace that it overlaps with one another. It's much different in communicating than the way we do here on Earth in the physical body.

Since all souls are born with measuring psychic gifts, this means you can also all train yourself to pay attention to the input you receive. You can train to give tarot or angel card readings for yourself or for others. It takes work to strip away the materialistic life that you have built up within your DNA in this lifetime. With practice and work, you can be just as capable of giving reads for yourself as a professional psychic reader can.

Those who are professional psychic readers or mediums find it difficult to read for themselves, since their judgment is clouded and not objective. This is why many will read with another reader to receive a read from someone who is not emotionally invested in their life. This is also why many psychics do not read for friends as it becomes a conflict of interest. They have emotion invested in their friend and may bend the read to favor the friend. In the end a false read is given and the friend is not helped. Sometimes it causes the ending of a friendship where the friend feels uncomfortable by what their psychic reader friend has relayed to them.

Searching for the right psychic reader can be challenging and much like searching for the right Doctor. Readers read in a variety of ways. Some are angel readers, some are fortune tellers, others channel messages from the other side, and some use objects, while others use nothing, but their own body. There will be a synastry between you and the reader that feels comfortable for you both. No reader should ever tell you what to do.

For example, they should never instruct you to leave a lover unless of course the lover is abusive. The role of an ethical reader is to simply guide you or inform you of what they are seeing about a particular person or situation in question. They should remain completely objective and neutral in your situation. An ethical reader would say something like, "If you stay with this person, the philandering will continue. It is up to you to decide on your next course of action." You have free will choice to decide what's best for you knowing this information.

I've had angel reads, psychic reads, tarot reads, channel reads, and intuitive reads. Those who use no divination tool, those who use boards, rocks or other devices. I love the craft and all points of view. I love the differing ways that others read. You gain different insights and perspectives with a different reader. It's a personal decision when choosing a reader to go with, just as you would in choosing a relationship. One person may love a reader that someone else did not gravitate towards. There is a synastry between reader and readee.

Sometimes others who enjoy the craft love to know what methods other readers use when reading cards. When using a card deck, I do not always use the three card spread. I've rarely if ever used the past-present-future spread or Celtic Cross spread. I don't have a pattern that I stick with when reading. I follow what my Spirit team is telling me through my Clairaudience channel. I pick the deck up as I'm saying, "I want to know about love for this person." I'm already shuffling before I've finished my sentence. For example, I will hear them say the number six. I nod, "Six. Okay, show me love". Some readers take the top 6 cards off when they're done shuffling. I shuffle for each 6 times until they have me stop on the card. This doesn't mean anyone should do it this way. You adopt the method that works accurately and best for you.

Ask your guides and angels for clarity when you're puzzled by their information. Request they show you signs and symbols to confirm what you're receiving from them. This is one way to determine if you're receiving accurate information or if it's your ego dominating the read. Every soul is born in tune to the other side and connected to God.

The more a human soul allows their physical surroundings to influence them, the further away from God and heavenly communication you go.

DO I VOLUNTEER INFORMATION TO OTHERS?

It is best to avoid volunteering psychic related information to others unless they've asked you for it. It's not particularly enjoyable watching others head for a cliff and not being able to say anything. You cannot interfere with others free will choice. They have to learn lessons on their own. I just keep it to myself unless I'm specifically asked if I'm seeing anything. There is the asking me what is the best course of action to take with a decision. I let them know what I'm getting. It goes through one ear out the other. They do the opposite, then come back to me to say, "Okay you were right, now what do I do? How do I get out of this?" It's uncomfortable to not come off as if you're shattering someone's dreams. I'm all for one going after what they want. They're very excited about something and you do not want to crush that for them. You see it being a dead end or not ending well, and they ask you about it. You have to be delicate in the delivery of what you're getting, while still allowing them their free will choice to make the ultimate decision while also being supportive too.

I'M HEARING VOICES TELLING ME THEY'RE GOING TO KILL ME!

Another common inquiry I receive is someone hearing voices that they are going to kill them. The inquiry comes to me wondering if it's a spirit on the other side. When one is hearing harmful voices, then this is typically the voice of ego. Spirits in Heaven only communicate with love, while the ego communicates in hate and negativity. If it's a demon possession, they would take over your entire soul and body, but those cases are extremely rare despite how common it seems in Hollywood horror films.

The harmful spirits in limbo mode that feed off a human soul's addictions merely prompt that human soul to dive harder into a particular addiction. They don't have the kind of power to whisper they're going to kill that soul. It would defeat their purpose as well, since their goal is simple. It is to get high through the human soul's addiction or vice.

If you're hearing negative voices speaking to you, it's important to first rule out if you've had a traumatic experience in your life. Sometimes traumatic events in one's life trigger negative self talk where it feels as if an entity or spirit is saying harmful negative things to you. Some post traumatic stress side effects cause one's mind to splinter into different selves where it feels as if it's not you saying particular harmful things, but an entity or spirit. It can happen months or even years after the traumatic event. Most people have had at least one traumatic event or circumstance they can recall through the duration of their life that stands out. It can be something seemingly insignificant to someone else, but which is not to you. Circumstances such as a love relationship breakup that left you wounded and depressed.

If the harmful voices are something that continues indefinitely, then it's best to seek out a mental health practitioner to adequately treat and/or diagnose the underlying cause. This can also rule out any deeper issues that might reside within you that need addressing and healing. The next step recommended is to go to a highly evolved healer, counselor, or therapist as you continue down your individual spiritual path.

Questions such as this one can be uncomfortable to answer, but the response is always the same. This type of question is best suited for a mental health professional. It's not my or anyone else's jurisdiction to diagnose a mental health issue, but left for someone medically qualified. It would be poor etiquette and bad practice on my part. I can only offer what my Spirit team relays to me, which is the same response for most common questions.

There is nothing wrong with seeking a professional who specializes with mental disorders. One's mental health is extremely vital, and being someone who has fragmented and split off into various selves as a child, I understand the importance of addressing it. This is in order to take care of it and examine the underlying cause, so that you can be clear minded. With practice, you will be able to decipher what are your guides and angels, and when your ego mind is playing tricks on you.

THE "OVER SOUL" AND "WALK-IN"

There is what some call an *Over Soul*. Your soul has a higher self and a lower self, and both are distinctively different selves. To some it would appear to be that all human souls have a split personality to an extent. This is depending on how often they vacillate from their higher to their lower self on any given day. Yet it's only one soul, not two. Everyone has a dark side and a light side.

There are cases where a soul will take over another soul's body at some point in their life. It is noticeable to others around them after this happens. The rare soul switching happens during a traumatic event such as a car accident or near death experience. This is where the soul switching takes place. Both souls agreed to have the switching prior to their Earthly life.

Once the soul switching takes place, others begin to notice the individual is not quite the same person they once knew. A pivotal event prompts the person to do a turnaround. They have suddenly changed their views; career, lovers, lifestyle choices and you name it! They almost seem like a stranger to those they are close to. There are elements that are the same since the memory banks of the previous soul have been transferred to the new soul. It's not like the new soul has amnesia. They're able to subconsciously reach into the memory banks of the previous soul's upbringing, but will not recall much. They will feel a detachment to it as if they weren't personally around for it. Some also call this a *Walk-In*.

Chapter Twelve

Psychic Timing

One of the questions most often asked in a psychic read is, "When?" When will a particular circumstance happen? They want an exact date as to when they will meet that lover, start that new career, or buy that house. This is understandable since you are in a human body and crave immediate material security. This physical comfort could come in the form of the great job, money, or awesome love for example. When these things do not seem to be forthcoming for a prolonged period of time, you might begin to grow permanently solemn, frustrated or disappointed. This state lowers your vibration which could block or delay the event from taking place. This energy certainly does not bring the event to you any more quickly. It is always best to remain optimistic and cheerful as that energy is what attracts in positive circumstances.

No psychic reader can necessarily predict when something is going to happen for someone. Those in Heaven who are relaying information to the psychic conduit live in a world without devices such as calendars and clocks. Those are manmade designs to give Earth life some resemblance of structure and order. There is no time that exists for Heaven in the way that human souls have made it on Earth. Therefore it's near impossible for spirit guides and angels to give a particular psychic conduit an accurate time to give to their client as to when an event will take place. Time is fluid to those in the spirit world, so when they see a human soul wanting to know when something will take place, they do their best to give an estimated time frame. This time frame should be taken with a grain of salt. There are a great many factors that can and will often delay something from happening with any time frame predicted.

There are psychics who nail timing more times than not, but for the most part it's challenging to nail timing. You are gambling with someone's free will choice, which is unpredictable. I've nailed timing in the past and witnessed it happen later. I have had the person I've relayed the information to come back to me a year later. This was in order to say that something I stated a year ago has come true for them. The majority of the time where I've read for others, I avoid giving timing answers, since that is a dangerous risk. It's rare to predict it on the mark because free will enters the equation. When someone asks for timing on something, I will rarely relay it unless I hear a month or date slam into my aura during a read. The circumstances where I offered accurate timing were voluntarily on my part because my Spirit team happened to be highlighting a month, day, or season through my clairaudience channel. I just included it as part of the read. If they say nothing as to when something will happen, then I will say "I don't know. Soon." There are reasons they're not telling the human soul. Sometimes information is on a need to know basis. Your ego wants to know when something is going take place. Your higher self is not interested in the when or how. It knows all is well and what is intended will be.

The timing that is given by a reader is the *probable timing* pending that you or other circumstances connected to your desire are not hindered by any of the party's free will. Free will is not taken seriously enough when it comes to a psychic read. Most human souls operate using free will choice. They rarely listen to their guides and angels. It is more about obtaining their desire immediately. For example, in a love read no one can predict the impulsive choices you or this potential lover might make on any given day. This alters what was originally predicted to happen.

There is a danger when a psychic gives someone a time frame as to when an event will happen. If the time frame the psychic gave comes and goes, then the one who was read for will debunk the psychic as being inaccurate or that it just isn't in the cards for them. Yet, months or even years down the line, it turns out that the event does eventually take place, but it is so far into the future that they've forgot all about the read to begin with.

When I was sixteen years old, my Spirit team had told me that I would be working in the entertainment business in the "near future". I didn't know what the near future was and I didn't ask them when exactly. I just knew without a doubt that it would happen. Of course, I didn't sit around waiting for it to land on my door step. I actively began researching the business at the library and investigating potential companies I could possibly work at.

To make a long story short, years passed and I was still researching and trying to get in. I grew frustrated and disheartened at times, but the desire to get in did not stop me. Weeks after my 23rd birthday, I was offered a position working for a major Hollywood actress at the time. This is to illustrate that I was shown this would happen at sixteen years old and in the near future. The event happened when I turned twenty-three. This dream came to fruition at full throttle about seven years *after* I clairvoyantly saw it coming initially. The point is that it did happen eventually. Can you imagine if I went to a psychic reader who told me, "You'll get into the entertainment business within the coming year?" I might have given up and said, "Oh they were wrong, that never happened." This is why psychic timing cannot always be accurately predicted on the mark. If it is, then keep an open mind that the reader is merely estimating the probable future. Just because the event doesn't take place when they said it would, does not necessarily mean that it won't ever happen.

One way to look at it is that a reader or your own guides and angels are informing you that something is indeed intended to happen. Don't worry yourself over the when and how it will happen. Otherwise you'll drive yourself into a mental obsession. This obsession is what lowers your vibration. When you are in a state of joy and contentment, in the here and now, then this raises your vibration. This then allows positive events to unfold, and even greater opportunities to reach you sooner than later.

I'm one of the most impatient people I know, so this is something I can relate to. I know what it's like to want to know when something is going to take place and how frustrating it can be when time has gone by and nothing has come to pass. Heaven says to trust, have patience, and keep the faith. Know that the path you're on is the way it is for a reason. The choices you've previously made have led you to the place you're currently in. What you desire will reveal itself to you at just the right time. Speaking from personal experience, I can attest that this is true.

Additionally, it's important to remember to follow the nudges, signs and guidance that you're Spirit team are putting in front of you. If they are constantly dropping the same signs in front of you to go to a different part of town you normally go to, or another store that is off your typical route, then trust that. It could be they are trying to orchestrate something beneficial for you. A psychic reader can rarely assist you with something like this. They might tell you that you're going to meet your next lover in October. October comes and goes and you wonder why it never happened. Were you sitting around at home hiding out between the day of your psychic read and October? This makes it impossible for any lover to find you unless that soul mate rings your doorbell like the postman or delivery person.

When a psychic informs you about a probable situation coming up, then keep an open mind. Take steps that can help it come along to you more readily. If this is a love partner entering the picture, then this means get outside and mix with other souls. Go out more often so that this wonderful lover can bump into you. Pay attention to your Spirit teams nudges on where to go if you're confused.

While out and about, if this potential lover approaches you and strikes up a friendly conversation, then let your guard down and throw on the charm with them. Smile, be engaging, warm and open. You might not be immediately aware that this person is the potential right away when they approach you. They might not be what you were originally envisioning or thought of, so you end up closing yourself off to someone who desires to engage with you in conversation.

Another important action step can be that it is

you who will approach this lover, instead of waiting for them to approach you. This is an easy step for an extroverted soul. If you're an introvert, then practice using your gifts of non-verbal telepathic communication on this potential. You can do this with a smile or by giving them a simple, "Hello." Pay attention to their body language and how responsive or unresponsive they are. This also means pay attention to your own body language. Do you stiffen up to a block of ice with an expressionless face when this person enters your vicinity and notices you?

This is a cold closed off world and some souls may have an automatic fight or flight response. They could be stunned that someone said hello to them let alone an attractive stranger. They might button up and turn away from you or give you a grunt of a response. Does that mean they're not interested? Not necessarily. When you're in tune to your surroundings, you can gauge whether someone is interested or not. Watch for the subtle cues in their body movement. Do they pull away from you feeling uninterested, angry or threatened? And do they suddenly soften and move back towards you with acknowledgment? Their movements may be subtle that you might not notice it right away. You assume they're not interested, when they may either be shy or thrown off that someone good looking is engaging with them.

Unless someone has been drinking in a bar to loosen up, most people are not used to others being nice to them, especially if you live in an overpopulated big city. Going to a bar or club with the goal of hoping to meet your long term relationship soul mate is a mistake and you'll wind up disappointed. Unless you're someone who loves hanging in a bar and looking for that like minded soul who enjoys the same drinking habits.

If you're a woman, you might have a traditional way of believing how relationships should form. This is where you prefer the guy approaches you and strikes up a conversation. That was the way things once were, but times are significantly different. Now both men and women have to do the work if they want to find a long term loving relationship. If you're a woman, then you approach him with a hello.

If you're interested in a same sex love relationship, then you have additional factors that come into play or ones that might cross your mind. They might be things such as, "What if I approach this person and they don't go my way?" Or what if they have a negative reaction to my sexuality? Of course, you would use precautions regardless of what your sexuality is when approaching a stranger. You're not going to blurt out: "Hey, I'm interested in you!" This method could work, but being subtle and polite in your approach can go a long way. This is where you are striking up a conversation as if it were a potential friend. You'll eventually pick up on enough energy vibrations off the other person to determine what their interest level is. There are human souls who are super sociable and friendly. It doesn't mean they're necessarily seeing you as a potential lover.

Your Spirit team is not going to drop the great lover at your doorstep if you're hiding out at home and you never go out to mingle. They're not going to drop an awesome career opportunity in your life if you've never sent your resume or credentials out to potential employers. Heaven helps those who help themselves. They help those they see are taking action steps to make it happen. When you're passionate and positively driven to achieve this desire, then it's that much quicker to arrive.

Chapter Thirteen

A Look at Some of
My Guides and Angels

There are seven main Spirit Guides and Angels that are part of my Spirit team. This includes my one main spirit guide and one guardian angel. They have both been with me since birth as everyone has this same deal. The other guides and angels around me came in one by one as I was growing up. They've remained permanently by my side in my current lifetime. There is also Saint Nathaniel who has been with me since around 2009. I was about to embark on a major transition once the healing from a relationship was complete from that particular connection. Saint Nathaniel is the tough love messages I feature in some of my works on humanity as a whole. He is the *warrior of light*, Wise One and task master who instructs most of the harsh stuff on humanity I sometimes bring up.

There is no set pattern that is consistent in how Guides and Angels communicate, because other factors play a part in that. It's a frequency that is shifting up and down all throughout the day and everyday depending on what's going on in your world. What your guides say is on a need to know basis. I've had letters sent to me by others who say their Guides are expressing frustration with them because they're not listening. This is not a Guide, but the ego taking over. An angel or heavenly guide is not going to tell someone that they're not listening and that they're tired of telling someone what to do. If you believe that they're telling you this, then you would hear the rest of the information and not just the frustration language. Scolding is a lower energy or the ego taking over. Angels use high vibrational words and energy when they communicate. They heal, comfort, inspire and guide delicately and positively. They have an endless reserve of patience so it's not likely an angel who is getting frustrated, but the ego.

It is also possible it can be a departed loved one, since they have a good measure of their human ego intact as they work to strip it away on the other side. If that's the case, then you'll want to request a higher vibrational guide and ask that the departed loved one be removed from the duties of assisting and guiding you.

There are other guides and angels that come in and out of my vicinity for different reasons, but the main seven, plus Saint Nathaniel, are the permanent team that never leave or are close by. There are occasions where I'm communicating specifically with one who I've addressed directly. Depending on what's going on or what the situation calls for, the right guide or angel steps forward. They take turns orchestrating certain events that are in my favor. One guide may be working on bringing the next love mate to me, while another is working on the career or work stuff. Their goal is to ensure that I stay on path teaching, writing, inspiring and entertaining. I have long lists of things that need to be said and done. One guide is not enough for all of it. There are times where they do speak in concert, except for Saint Nathaniel who works separately with me.

The names of my Spirit Guides and Angels around me are Luke, Enoch, Veronica, Matthew, Jeremiah, Samuel and Jacob. Saint Nathaniel sometimes known as Bartholomew leads the pack.

Luke is my main Spirit Guide and has been since my human birth in this lifetime. His main role with me was and has been my entire work and career life to date. Every job and work position I ever received since I was seventeen were all part of the plan to gain additional tools and knowledge that would lead to the role I am in now. Luke has been instrumental in this process and continues to be so. He works closely with Archangel Gabriel and

Archangel Uriel who comes in when it comes to my writing and promoting my work.

Veronica is my main Guardian Angel and has been since birth. She has been the front and center angel that has kept me on a healthy path. I knew from the early age of eight the importance of exercise and health. This was instilled in me primarily from Veronica. There were times where I indulged in addictions that would lead to one poor situation after another. Both Luke and Veronica would scream through the thud to get me back on path as soon as possible. Luckily, I listened to my Guides and Angels, otherwise I may have checked out early.

As I grew to know my guides and angels, I discovered some interesting historical facts about them that they did not reveal immediately. The reason they often withhold information from you is for a variety of reasons. One of them is that sometimes it's a 'need to know' basis. Other times it can be that you may not be in a position to accept the answer.

Saint Nathaniel

Saint Nathaniel is one of the many Ascended Masters on the other side. Ascended Masters are also Saints who often act as spiritual teachers and guides to advancing or evolving student souls on Earth for specific purposes. This is when you are ready to take on a more serious role in this lifetime that entails helping others through communication, leading, teaching and inspiring. It is not uncommon for Wise Ones to have guides who are ascended masters. Nathaniel started popping in for me in a regular appearance in 2009-a catastrophic year for me personally. It was crucial in that it was the ending of another chapter part of my life. It was the final chapter of all my years up to that point. Nathaniel knew where I would be embarking to next, which was an entirely different book, rather than the next chapter. The life lessons, class and karmic debt were wrapping themselves up. My soul vibration was rising to a higher degree. I was climbing out of the confinement of my material body.

Nathaniel instructed that I move into the role of the empowering teacher that all of my guides had been showing me for the ten years prior, but my ego denied this. My work life would be shifting and I would go through a powerful spiritual transformation. This is described in my book, *Reaching for the Warrior Within*. My Spirit Guide Luke had informed me that in November 2010 I experienced what someone might consider to be a near death experience while enduring a physical work out injury. This lasted for a millisecond in Earth time. Something shifted and turned in me where I would never be the same again after that month. This was simultaneous with the death of my father within that same month. This marked where my soul was freed and my former karmic debt officially paid off. I merged effortlessly and immediately into the role of a Warrior of Light full time. The change happened so gradually and fluidly by sheer magic. It was as if some strong force did something to my soul that profoundly shifted something within me at that point. I was awakened! My state of mind has been awesome ever since.

Saint Nathaniel appeared in 2009 just as the transition was about to happen in order to start aiming me in that direction. He knew what was coming. When I was on the other side, he and I, along with my other guides all discussed the agreement that included when they would reveal themselves to me during my Earthly run.

In the summer of 2011, I asked who was guiding me with all of this new stuff that I seemed to know involuntarily. He said his name was, Nathaniel. He didn't seem like the usual suspects around me, but instead came off quite stern and authoritative. His language had a biblical tone and was decoded into English in order for me to understand. It's like talking to someone with an accent. I asked why he sounds as if he is ancient. He informed me that he is not one of my guardian angels, but a hierarchy Saint and Ascended Master. He has been a crucial force in any and all words I utter that are aligned with humanity. Humanity is in desperate need of a real awakening. That is obviously coming from Nathaniel since before that point I could care less.

There was another spirit with the same energy as Nathaniel who started communicating with me around the same time. He said his name was, Bartholomew. Months later, I realized that Nathaniel was and is Bartholomew. I didn't understand the point of the interchangeable name. Nathaniel/Bartholomew ushered in the important messages in my previous spiritual books, *Warrior of Light: Messages from my Guides and Angels* and *Empowering Spirit Wisdom*. When those works were complete, he informed me in greater detail who he was in a human life. This was in order to not distract me from the work of those particular books.

Saint Nathaniel is from the tribe of the Wise Ones. He is known to some on Earth as one of the three Wise men who brought gifts for the celebration of the birth of Jesus Christ. To some he is known as one of the Twelve Apostles. It was suddenly all being pieced together for me. Some on Earth also knew Saint Nathaniel as Bartholomew in those ancient days. Saint Nathaniel is from the Realm of the Wise One and was a Wise Man on Earth. He's worked with Christ and was a well known astrologer in those days. All of these mark the traits of someone who is a Wise One. His authoritative teaching tone when he speaks, display a highly evolved Ascended Master.

When further discovering this information, my Guides and Angels pointed out who they were. They are prophets, angels and teachers from what some consider the biblical years. They have been referenced often in various philosophical texts.

Many prophets come from the Realm of the Wise One, so I did not find this surprising that they were my guides. Wise Ones in human form travelling with the big guns is not uncommon. Incidentally, Saint Nathaniel was known to have carried the Book of Matthew when he was a human soul. Matthew and Nathaniel are the guides that work with me. My main spirit guide, Luke, was considered to be an intelligent writer and scholar during biblical days in human form. He has a section featured in the Bible called the Book of Luke. One of my Guardian Angels, Veronica, wiped the face of Jesus before the crucifixion according to some texts. She allegedly appeared as human to the physical eyes which is not uncommon of an angel.

My Spirit Guide, Enoch, is a Wise One who incarnated on Earth to teach about humanity. He wrote books about the sacred knowledge of creation. Enoch was a profit who walked with God in Genesis and never wavered even though some ridiculed him. He resurrected when he crossed over. His great grandson was Noah of the famous, "Noah's Ark" story. He is a descendant from Adam of the "Adam and Eve" story. I went to Bible school as a young child, but it did not have a lasting or profound effect on me. As someone with ADD and ADHD in a human body, it is challenging for me to retain information, especially memories from Childhood. Remembering the names of those listed in the Bible from that period are impossible. This is why I rely on my Spirit team to filter in the information naturally. My eyes narrowed with skepticism and soon evaporated as they pointed out that they are indeed mentioned in the book. It was only after I discovered who was around me that I noticed the irony. Leave it to me to bring in the big guns from the spirit world.

Questions from Readers About Spirit Guides & Angels

Q: What is the best way to contact guides when you are having trouble connecting through meditation?

A: Spirit Guides and Angels are by your side the instant you call them. You do not need to do any special invocation or meditation to communicate with them. The reason why meditating is effective is because it puts you in a calm and relaxed state. You are more apt to receiving their messages clearly when you are in that space, rather than stressed or distracted.

Q: Can you explain blinks of light? I've been seeing them for years. Not sure if it is guides.

A: There are angel trails or lights that may show up in one's peripheral vision if their third eye is open. If this is the case, then you are seeing them clairvoyantly. They do appear as lights for some people.

Q: Do guides work through numbers to get your attention? When you see the same sequence of numbers, could it be your guide?

A: Angels and Spirit Guides communicate with you in many ways and yes through numbers and symbols is one way.

Q: With meditation, how do we know if we are connecting with our guides and it's not our imagination or wishes?

A: They will use the pronoun *"You"* while your own thoughts and ego use the pronoun *"I"*. Your higher self is 100% psychic while your lower self is not. Every human soul communicates with them in varying ways whether they are aware of it or not.

They mainly communicate through their 'clair channels'. If you are receiving positive messages and nudges repeatedly, then it is likely them. These messages will come to you more than three times. Your ego or lower self will conjure up something once and discard it. If your ego is being repetitive or 'obsessing', it is prompting you to do something that you know is not good for you. The messages or guidance from Spirit will be urging you to do something that will positively benefit you or someone else.

Q: Could Children's imaginary friends be Spirit Guides?

A: Children are more adept at communicating with Spirit Guides. They don't hold lower self-judgments the way Adults have learned to do. Children know more about acceptance and love than any adult. Adults are damaged Children who were lured into a certain way of thinking due to their surroundings and upbringing. Children view things in a purer way and use less of their ego. The ego blows up to the size of a football field once Adults get a hold of it.

Q: I'm new to this, what are guides?

A: A guide is a spirit on the other side who is assigned to you through the duration of your lifetime on Earth. Their purpose is to help, nudge and guide you along the right path steering you away from poor choices if you pay attention to them. They do not make your decisions for you, but they do intervene when you are going off course. They are essentially your right hand confidante who knows everything about you including your thoughts, feelings and needs. They do not help you fulfill needs that are against your greater good such as hanging around the wrong people, doing drugs and alcohol or absorbing yourself in toxic addictions. In fact, they nudge you to steer clear of bad vices. Your ego is so powerful that it ignores the wisdom your guide has for you.

Q: When I meditate I see faces of people I do not know. Are these guides?

A: They may be your guide or an angel, but not always. You may be outwardly projecting your subconscious mind. This may prompt your mind to display shadows. This is a sign of an activated clairvoyance channel.

Q: How do you tell the difference between a Guide versus an Angel?

A: A guide is typically someone who had an Earthly life, but went through advanced training on the other side to be a pure Spirit Guide for a human soul during its Earth life. Guardian Angels were never human in my experience, but always a spirit. They may temporarily appear human for a purpose or to avert you from danger or crises and then disappear.

Q: Can guides heal you with your body and mind?

A: Some guides have specific specialties that they work with you on like love, health, career, etc. They heal your body and mind so that you are operating from your higher self and more able to communicate with God.

Q: Are we able to call more than one Guide for help with different projects or problems? Is it always necessary to call them?

A: You can call on as many Guides and Angels as you like. When they have worked with you on a specific issue and there is no need for anymore assistance, then they move on to help other souls calling out for them. Your main Spirit Guide and Guardian Angel are always around you and never leave. They guide and help you along your life path. However, it is necessary to ask for their help, as they cannot intervene with your free will unless you have asked them to.

Q: How long do you experience meditation before you feel your guides' presence?

A: To feel them it can take anywhere from 5 to 15 minutes of meditation or by being still and relaxed. Breathing is important as it not only relaxes you, but delivers oxygen into every cell in your body allowing you to be a fine tuned receptive communication tool with them. It's like clearing the static of a telephone line.

Q: I get those voices that tell me what's going on. It's a voice, a feeling and a twinge in my heart area all at once. They validate questions at times, sometimes they validate before I have the questions. Is that my Guide?

A: If the messages you are receiving this way end up coming true, then yes they are your guide or your angel.

Q: Do the deceased watch us do things like taking a shower?

A: They do not watch you shower, dress or have sex. They do not have that kind of attraction or interest. They see your soul as light and feeling. If that gives you peace of mind to know you're not being watched every time you strip down. Those on the other side are not Peeping Toms. The only exception may be an Earth bound spirit who chose not to cross over and is basically hanging out in limbo mode. They get a rush out of re-enacting the same activity with a human soul indefinitely, or until they make the move into the light to be purified.

Q: How can I find out the name of my Spirit Guide and Guardian Angel?

A: Knowing their name varies from person to person. There are times where they do not go by any name, specifically your guardian angel who has never been in human form. Some may make up a name so that you feel more comfortable able to address them in some way. It doesn't matter how you address them. You can ask them to tell you their name. Ask them to continue to show you signs and confirmation of what it is. Then start paying attention to the signs and symbols in your surroundings. Perhaps in the following week or so you keep running into people with the name of "James" and you see that name out of nowhere on Billboards, signs etc. That's one way they can communicate with you.

Q: How do I communicate with the Archangels?

A: Communicating with the Archangels happen the same way you communicate with the angels, guardian angels, ascended masters, spirit guides and deceased loved ones. Being in a meditative state helps since it brings your soul into a more calm and receptive place. When you are calm and feeling uplifting joy without any chemicals is the most efficient way. This is when your energy vibration is raised closer to Heaven and you receive clear divine communication more effortlessly. When you are under stress, experiencing negative emotions, or on heavy alcohol, bad foods or other toxic vices, then this creates restrictions, which form blocks that clog up these etheric phone cords that connect you to Spirit. Of course they are always communicating with you, but are you hearing them?

Q: Why do people who do bad things or hurt others have great success in life or seem to have it easier? How come those who do good get nowhere?

A: One of the things is that some of these perceived bad people know they are going to get what they want no matter what. Their intention to getting what they want is so great and they are so optimistic and sure of themselves about it that they manifest it. They are not going to get away with something bad. If they do, it will be short-lived. They will be stopped. The angels see the goodness in ALL people whether that person is good or bad. They do not place them into separate categories. There are guides and spirits who are not egoless and are doing different work in Heaven. They see the behavior of mankind and do not take it lightly.

Each individual case would have to be examined to give you the reasons why as it's not that cut and dry. If a good person is not manifesting, but instead living in frustration over it, then that is what they are attracting to themselves.

Q: I am starting to open my heart and eyes to new vibrations and I am trying to have a connection with angels by sending them my love. The more I do this I seem to be getting small white feathers left in front of me. At work, at home, in the street, and even one in my hair. What's going on or am I starting to be weird? It's almost daily now. I'm not sure what to do so I feel happy to pick it up and say thank you. Should I be doing something? I think I have made myself look strange enough for now, but I had to ask someone and it's not something I can bring up around people I know.

A: You are opening yourself up more to the light and to the angels. When someone is making an attempt to communicate or connect with the angels sometimes they wonder if they are being heard. Some don't visually see the angels in front of them and so they may question whether or not they are being heard. The angels have connected with you the second you have put out the intention to communicate with them. They try various ways of making contact with you, either through your various senses or in other ways through numbers and symbols. This is how you communicate with Spirit.

We have various ways of communicating such as by phone, email or texting. Since those on the other side can't just pick up the phone, they use creative ways of communicating as we will too when we cross over. We won't need things like phones or computers. One of the big ways that angels like to let you know that they are hearing you is they love to drop white feathers around. You suddenly start finding them in places where it doesn't seem feasible for it to suddenly show up. They tend to do it quite a bit with those who are fervently trying to connect with them. They will do it when someone is desperately needing an answer to something specific and wondering if they're being heard. You are. This is their way of telling you, *'We hear you loud and clear.'* There is nothing you need to do, but accept this love that they are showering upon you. You can even save the feather in a special place as a gift if you choose.

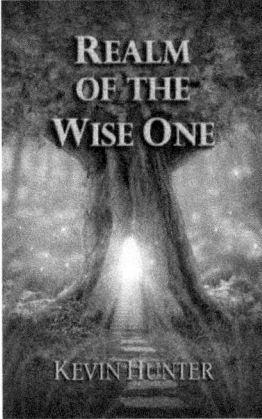

Realm of the Wise One

Available in paperback and e-book

Excerpt Sample

The Wise Ones who incarnate in a human body are natural born leaders and teachers. They're the generals of an army or a soldier in combat. They are the pot stirrers that bring on significant change through their sometimes seeming aggression. Wise One's are the darkest breed in the angelic spiritual Realm. Their presence is darker, tougher and even more sinister than any of the other realms. Wise Ones do not hold back and can be uncensoring at times. They have foul mouths cursing and cussing like sailors, but yet teach and fight in the name of the Light. Their personalities and demeanor comes off rougher around the edges than other folks. Some of them are quite intimidating in the way that they carry themselves and appear. Some are brawny and strong such as history's soldiers at war. There are the Wise Ones who might appear small, yet when you examine them closely you'll notice their body is quite strong.

When in doubt, one of the best ways to determine who is a Wise One is in their eyes. Their eyes are large, stunning, dark, intensely piercing and penetrating. Many of them never get used to others gushing over the beauty of their eyes. When some Wise Ones age in human years, they may develop significant lines under their eyes more than someone else might. You see this in the wise image of a professor or teacher. Do not be misled by the Wise Ones in human body who appear frail or ancient, as they are anything but delicate.

Wise Ones have a significant sized ego, but not quite as large as the Incarnated Elementals. They are also critical and judgmental about most everything around them. Generally the judgments are surrounding those that lack respect or are without proper etiquette. It's this kind of teaching toughness where no guff is allowed. They have no problem flipping back and forth from keeping to themselves to working independently. Hard work is a big deal for Wise Ones. They at times have opinions that they know are gold while the rest are ignored. To say they can be self-righteous at times is an understatement. "It's my way or the high way," would be a Wise One talking.

The soul of a Wise One is an innate loner who fights and hunts. They feel little to no shame or guilt in their actions or words even if it's out of line. They have a job to do and nothing will get in their way. This personality trait is part of their soul make-up and exists while living in an Earthly life.

Wise Ones are awesome manifestors, spell casters, psychics and all knowing spirits in human bodies. They will bring in and deny anything effortlessly depending on how they channel the energies. Wise Ones could be a warlock or witch type. They have a great fascination for Wicca. They are attracted to and explore the dark arts. They also have a special affinity to movies on magic, manifestation and sorcery. This might be entertainment such as Harry Potter, American Horror Story: The Coven, Hocus Pocus, Sword and the Stone, or the Chronicle. All Wise Ones on the other side use spell casting and magic. This is regardless of what form they take and whether it is in the form of a Warlock, Knight, Witch, Wizard, High Priest or Priestess or Hunter. This is the way things work on the other side even if they do not partake in it as a human soul. A human soul would need to suspend disbelief to comprehend the ways the spirits move about on the other side. Witch or warlock can be either male or female. They incarnate from the Realm of the Wise One. I fall into the breed of the Hunter. Yet, the Hunter is still part of the tribe of the Wise Ones and has the same capabilities as the Warlock, Priest or any other element from the world of the Wise Ones.

Wise Ones also come in the guises of Church leaders such as priests and ministers. They're also the task master professors in the education system. They're usually strict, brooding, serious, but boasting of love and compassion intertwined from within. God forbid they show this! When the Wise One speaks, he means business! The Wise One can command an army of thousands, like Martin Luther King Jr. or stand on a concert stage in front of thousands in popular culture like Bono from the rock group U2. The musicians that fall into the Wise One category are the ones that have higher purposes to help humanity in some way beyond the music. Many of them tend to be the rockers while the pop stars of today are more of the Incarnated Elemental variety.

Tending to moodiness, being difficult and appearing with intense dark eyes, Wise Ones "know it all" and may not know how they do when you ask them. Wise Ones incarnated from the other side are Claircognizant in a bigger way than others. This is a sense of knowing the correct answers to something without any prior training. They receive heavenly guidance effortlessly through their crown chakra above their mind. They're the ones that others go to for advice or assistance. People learn to trust the Wise One as they are one of the most trustworthy people around, but just avoid getting on their bad side or rubbing them the wrong way. Those ready to move to the next plateau spiritually in their soul's growth find themselves attracted to a Wise One and take heed of their wisdom. The lesser evolved or superficial souls may feel threatened by the Wise One or find them to be dull or on the boring side. They may also find that they cannot relate to them socially or are intimidated by them. These are the human souls that are consumed by poor media and life choices. They're the ones prone to drama and gossip, which the Wise One shuts down and rarely resorts to. The Wise One has a holier than thou stance in the presence of those less evolved.

The Wise Ones are used to attracting in people from all walks of life. Many befriend them for their knowledge and what they can gain in that arena. Some of those that latch onto the Wise One develop an immediate heightened delusion that they are close best friends with the Wise One, when in reality they are mere acquaintances. Danger lies when a co-dependent human soul latches onto the Wise One for a friendship in order to simply dump their problems on them or impress them. This is a forced and unbalanced friendship where the other person is using the Wise One to pour their drama issues onto them on a regular basis, or probe them for constant help and information. The Wise One is usually hip to what is taking place and they know that this connection dynamic will eventually end. They are so used to stepping in to assist others with their problems, that they must guard themselves that boundaries are not crossed and friendships are not forced with them. Unlike the Incarnated Angels who will feel guilt and fear about cutting someone toxic out of there life, the Wise One doesn't observe those feelings when removing a low vibration human soul from their vicinity. The Wise One is easily irritated and rubbed the wrong way that flicking harsh energies off their shoulders is a regular occurrence. A Wise One needs to be careful on how they direct their energy, since it flows through them almost effortlessly. It might cause upsetting situations in their lives for them, or for others, when they direct and channel this energy negatively. When someone doesn't follow their lead, the Wise Ones are the souls that have the temper in the Spirit world. They have to be careful how they channel this aggression since it will create a catastrophe when intertwined with their magic manifestation capabilities. Both the Wise Ones and the Incarnated Elementals have the greater egos and temper than any of the other Realms. However, the Wise Ones have the greater tempers while the Incarnated Elementals have the greater ego and demand for attention. You would think they would go hand and hand, but they are quite different.

Wise Ones are close to and drawn to the Incarnated Elementals and vice versa. The Incarnated Elementals are on the upbeat side and drawn to the serious leadership of the Wise Ones. It is an interesting match of opposites attract. You have the outgoing or childlike Elemental, with a darker, serious and withdrawn Wise One. A great deal of my serious love relationships have been with Incarnated Elementals! This goes without saying that some of my close friendships are with these out of sorts Elementals too. The Wise Ones bring order and discipline to the Elementals, while the Elementals help the Wise Ones relax, lighten up and enjoy life a little.

Wise Ones are attracted to darker material and even entertainment or lifestyles. It's not uncommon for them to have experimented with everything under the sun including and even fallen into addictions with drugs, alcohol, cigarettes and sex pursuits. They might also be prone to self-medicating in other ways beyond this if they can get their hands on it. They have no problem experimenting with all that life has to offer even if it's harmful. It subconsciously feeds their need to understand how something works. The colors within their soul are bright able to absorb the human experience more than any other. The addictive behavior is there under the surface, but it's not usually long lasting the way it would be with an Elemental indulging in their drink for an entire Earthly life. When Wise Ones realize their calling, they immediately pull themselves up by their bootstraps and dive in like a confident soldier. Wise Ones are the fighters, soldiers and hunters from the other side in the literal sense. Some wear the knight armor, others wear the cloak, and some carry the bow and arrow (as described in the beginning of the book). Wise Ones are the professors, the Saints, the leaders of change, the generals, sergeants, and soldier's in the army and marines in the navy. Because the Wise One's often have to be right, they might be the defiant soldier or marine. However, they are typically considered one of the best by those in charge, therefore it's overlooked. The Wise One has the stance that they have a job to do. They have no need or desire to be micro managed. With that said, most of them are entrusted with the bigger missions in combat by their superiors.

In fact some of the most notable Wise Ones are the popular Saints and Prophets in the world's history. People such as Saint Louis, who was already made King of France at the age of twelve. He also got his hands dirty by going to battle with the other soldiers. There was Saint Vladimir of Kiev in the 900 years A.D. In the beginning of his rule he was considered someone with an ugly temper and did some horrible things such as human sacrifices and obtaining hundreds of concubines. At one point he turned against paganism and went through a personal transformation that led him to be a "man of faith". His horrible reputation was quickly transformed and others began to refer to him as Vladimir the Great. The history books are filled with Wise Ones who started out with a bad reputation and who are not exactly the friendliest people on the planet right off the bat, but they end up transforming into more of a spiritual calling and following. Make no mistake that they did not necessarily change to being sweet as pie, but their fights and intense energy were transferred into more religious, spiritual and faith based fights. Wise Ones who come in the guises of Popes and Bishops would be the one granting the Saint title to the Wise One individual who has made an impact towards humanity and history.

When a Wise One enters the room, others notice. They will come off quiet, intense or with an air of superiority even though they're not trying to convey that on purpose. No one could pull off that act day after day until the end of their lifetime. It is part of their innate nature. It is how their energy light is on the other side. Those who do not know them in a personal way will immediately assume that the Wise One is conceited or icy cold. They may describe them to others by using an unpleasant curse word. As one takes the time to befriend and get to know the Wise One, they will discover they have to put in some effort since Wise Ones do not become instant friends with anybody. They have a protruding wall of distrust of others around them that must be scaled gradually over time before they open up. The opening up takes awhile and even then you feel like you don't really know them. Their opening up will be in short bursts, before they become comfortable enough to pour endless words over someone.

Those who initially had found the Wise One difficult and rough edged at the first encounter will notice a different side to them as they become closer. They will realize they've made an error in judgment and that the Wise One is indeed one of the coolest and most loyal people they know. They come to find that the Wise One is charismatic and warm when they're called to engage in social situations and put on that politician energy. Most of the Wise Ones personality is of a dark, depressed energy keeping to themselves. This is not out of shyness, but out of disinterest in superficial small talk. They dislike idle chit-chat and gossip and will rarely strike up a conversation out of the blue with someone in an elevator unless they're asked a question. In fact, they may step away from strangers in an elevator or anywhere for that matter. They want the bullet points when someone is addressing them or in a meeting, but when you ask them a question, they will give you a novel of an answer.

A Wise One might be pushed into the role of giving speeches rallying up the masses with their work, but some of them are uncomfortable on a stage. If this is the case, they may have other astrological influences that point to this. There might also have been crucial incidents that happened within their upbringing and development of their current life as a human soul that resulted in a fear of the stage. These things play a part within the Wise One who might be uncomfortable getting in front of the masses. You must strip the soul of their human ego learning's to get to the heart of their realm. You're looking at what they tend to exude overall.

Wise Ones often feel gypped that human souls have lied and caused so many preventable issues. Mankind has turned others against spiritual belief concepts to no belief at all with great success! This is one of the reasons Wise Ones incarnate. They are not instructing and authoritative out of malice, but to correct the bully's behavior.

Wise Ones either appear much older than their years or much younger than their years. They rarely look exactly their age. In fact, throughout most of their life they may comment that others come off shocked when they find out how old they truly are. When I was 21, I looked like I was 12. When I was 35, people thought I was 24 and in College. The Wise Ones have an interesting appearance where there age is difficult to detect. The Wise Ones who have always appeared much older than their years gives them the look of many lifetimes etched into their face. Those who have always appeared younger than their human age have that elusive, mysterious quality of centuries gone by. They fit the image of the vampire, which is another favorite mythological character of a Wise One. If vampire, Count Dracula, were real he would be a Wise One. He's got the gothic darkness in him. He's got the romanticism in his search for love and the dangerous anger when crossed.

Although a Wise One may come out of hiding to rally up the masses when it's called for, generally they are more on the reclusive side. Wise Ones may be accused of being cynical. This is someone who has distaste for the direction humankind has been going in. The Wise Ones may appear misanthropic, but in truth they have exceedingly high expectations from human souls. They see humanity as a whole has not got their act together after all of these centuries. They're still fighting and demanding attention or paying attention to less important causes. They believe humanity doesn't have a high standard of professionalism and decorum in their day to day connections with other human beings. Wise Ones are the taskmasters and disciplinarians after all and when a student defies their instructions, this will rise the Wise One into irritation. They will more or less cast that soul out of their vicinity. This makes them seem anti-social at times, yet they are far from it. They simply direct and channel their energy towards those souls who are ready to listen. They do not direct their energy towards anyone or anything that doesn't need to be.

This detached coolness can turn off, attract or repel other human souls. Lower energies are uncomfortable with someone who is not like the others. Wise Ones do not refuse conformity on purpose. They have lived through so many lifetimes and in the Spirit World that most of that nature is engrained into their human soul.

Where an Incarnated Angel may find it difficult to say "no" or will go out of their way to assist most anyone in need, the Wise One and the Incarnated Elementals with their ego expect others to work for it. The Wise Ones specifically don't have a problem saying no, even if they did in adolescence. Once they come into their own, if they hadn't at an early age, they will start asserting themselves. Wise Ones have a fine tuned detector where they can immediately tell if someone is of honor or not within a minute or two. I know very few Wise Ones who have actually had constant run-ins with someone of less integrity. Usually the calls I get from being slighted by others on a regular basis come from other human souls, Incarnated Angels, Star people, and Elementals.

Wise Ones on the other side are the many that greet the soul who is crossing over from the Earth plane. The soul has questions within them, which the Wise One on the other side answers. Family and friends greet the departed soul on the other side. It's the Wise One who is there with them to chime in and answer the questions from the newly departed soul. The Wise One helps them make amends for crimes they've committed on Earth, along with Archangel Jeremiel, and that soul's Guide and Angel.

When I asked why souls are tested at times. My team said, "If we don't test them, then how will they learn?" This is much like when you go to school and have to take a test in order to gain knowledge. Who do you think is executing these test orders? Many come from the Realm of the Wise One.

Wise Ones will have most of the traits discussed in this book if not all. If you find that you fall into maybe half of the traits without question, then it's possible you fall into one of the many blended realms that have some Wise One in them. For instance, the Mystic Angel is half Wise One and half Incarnated Angel.

ALSO BY KEVIN HUNTER

Warrior of Light
Empowering Spirit Wisdom
Darkness of Ego
Realm of the Wise One
Transcending Utopia
Reaching for the Warrior Within
Spirit Guides and Angels
Soul Mates and Twin Flames
Raising Your Vibration
Divine Messages for Humanity
Connecting with the Archangels
Monsters and Angels
The Seven Deadly Sins
Love Party of One
Twin Flame Soul Connections
A Beginner's Guide to the Four Psychic Clair Senses
Attracting in Abundance
Tarot Card Meanings
Abundance Enlightenment
Living for the Weekend
Ignite Your Inner Life Force
Awaken Your Creative Spirit
The Essential Kevin Hunter Collection

The Essential Kevin Hunter Collection
Available in Paperback and E-book

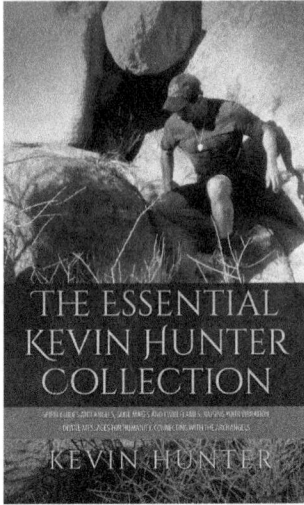

THE ESSENTIAL
KEVIN HUNTER
COLLECTION

Featuring the following books:
Warrior of Light, Empowering Spirit Wisdom, Darkness of Ego,
Spirit Guides and Angels, Soul Mates and Twin Flames, Raising
Your Vibration, Divine Messages for Humanity, and Connecting
with the Archangels.

Attracting in Abundance

Opening the Divine Gates to Inviting in Blessings and Prosperity Through Body, Mind, and Soul Spirit

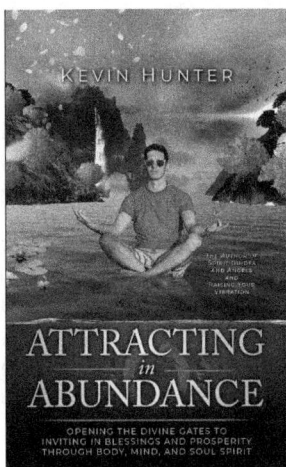

When you hear the word abundance, you may equate it to being blessed with a plentiful overflowing amount of money that equates to a big lottery win. Having enough money to survive comfortably enough on this physical plane is part of obtaining abundance, but it's not the destination and purpose to thrive for. You could work hard to make enough money to the point you are set for life, but that won't necessarily equate to happiness. Achieving a content satisfied state of joy and serenity starts with examining your soul's state and overall well-being. When that's in place, then the rest will follow.

Attracting in Abundance combines practical and spirit wisdom surrounding the nature of abundance. This is something that most everyone can get on board with because all human beings desire physical comforts, blessings, and prosperity, regardless of their personal values and belief systems. *Attracting in Abundance* is broken up into three parts to help move you towards inviting abundance into your life on all levels. "Part One" contains some no-nonsense lectures surrounding the philosophies, concepts, and debates on the laws of attracting in abundance. "Part Two" is the largest of the sections geared towards fine tuning the soul into preparing for abundance. "Part Three" is the final lesson plan to help crack open the gates of abundance with various helpful tidbits, guidance, and messages as well as the blocks that can prevent abundance from coming in.

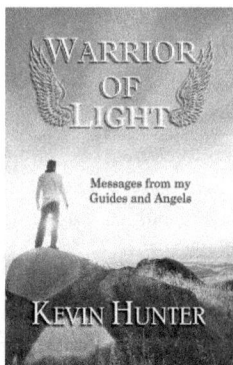

WARRIOR OF LIGHT
Messages from my Guides and Angels

There are legions of angels, spirit guides, and departed loved ones in heaven that watch and guide you on your journey here on Earth. They are around to make your life easier and less stressful. Learn how you can recognize the guidance of your own Spirit team of guides and angels around you. Author, Kevin Hunter, relays heavenly guided messages about getting humanity, the world, and yourself into shape. He delivers the guidance passed onto him by his own Spirit team on how to fine tune your body, soul and raise your vibration. Doing this can help you gain hope and faith in your own life in order to start attracting in more abundance.

EMPOWERING SPIRIT WISDOM
A Warrior of Light's Guide on Love, Career and the Spirit World

Kevin Hunter relays heavenly, guided messages for everyday life concerns with his book, *Empowering Spirit Wisdom*. Some of the topics covered are your soul, spirit and the power of the light, laws of attraction, finding meaningful work, transforming your professional and personal life, navigating through the various stages of dating and love relationships, as well as other practical affirmations and messages from the Archangels. Kevin Hunter passes on the sensible wisdom given to him by his own Spirit team in this inspirational book.

DARKNESS OF EGO

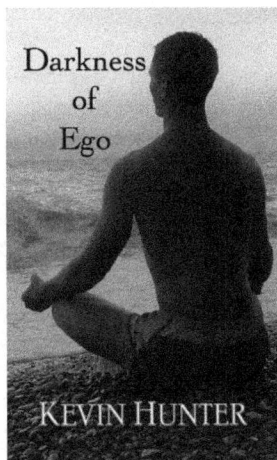

In *Darkness of Ego*, author Kevin Hunter infuses some of the guidance, messages, and wisdom he's received from his Spirit team surrounding all things ego related. The ego is one of the most damaging culprits in human life. Therefore, it is essential to understand the nature of the beast in order to navigate gracefully out of it when it spins out of control. Some of the topics covered in *Darkness of Ego* are humanity's destruction, mass hysteria, karmic debt, and the power of the mind, heaven's gate, the ego's war on love and relationships, and much more.

REACHING FOR THE WARRIOR WITHIN

Reaching for the Warrior Within is the author's personal story recounting a volatile childhood. This led him to a path of addictions, anxiety and overindulgence in alcohol, drugs, cigarettes and destructive relationships. As a survival mechanism, he split into many different "selves". He credits turning his life around, not by therapy, but by simultaneously paying attention to the messages he has been receiving from his Spirit team in Heaven since birth.

REALM OF THE WISE ONE

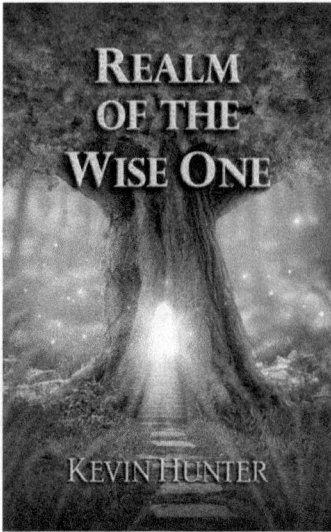

In the Spirit Worlds and the dimensions that exist, reside numerous kingdoms that house a plethora of Spirits that inhabit various forms. One of these tribes is called the Wise Ones, a darker breed in the spirit realm who often chooses to incarnate into a human body one lifetime after another for important purposes.

The *Realm of the Wise One* takes you on a magical journey to the spirit world where the Wise Ones dwell. This is followed with in-depth and detailed information on how to recognize a human soul who has incarnated from the Wise One Realm. Author, Kevin Hunter, is a Wise One who uses the knowledge passed onto him by his Spirit team of Guides and Angels to relay the wisdom surrounding all things Wise One. He discusses the traits, purposes, gifts, roles, and personalities among other things that make up someone who is a Wise One. Wise Ones have come in the guises of teachers, shaman, leaders, hunters, mediums, entertainers and others. *Realm of the Wise One* is an informational guide devoted to the tribe of the Wise Ones, both in human form and on the other side.

TRANSCENDING UTOPIA

Available in Paperback and E-book

Transcending Utopia is packed with practical and spirit knowledge that focuses on enhancing your life through empowering divinely guided spiritual related teachings, inspiration, wisdom, guidance, and messages. The way to accelerate existence on Earth towards Utopia is if every person on the planet resided in their soul's true nature, which is in a state of all love, joy, and peace. The ultimate Nirvana is surpassing that perfection through methods that a limited consciousness could ever dream possible. This is the exceptional glory your soul was born into before the dense turbulence of Earthly life enveloped and suffocated you.

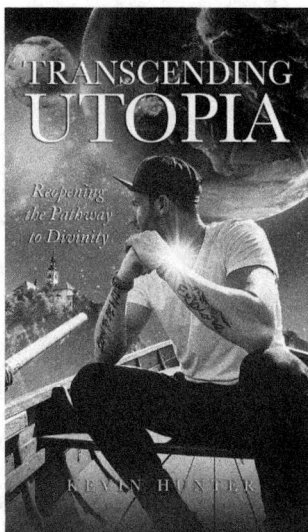

Transcending Utopia is to go beyond your limits and travel outside of the generic mundane materialistic achievement that human beings taught one another to thrive for. A utopian society is where everything is perfectly blissful on all levels according to the sanctified values you were born with. The sensations connected to how flawless everything feels in that moment reveals the authentic perfection you were made from. Utopia is the ideal paradise as imagined in one's dreams that seems to be inaccessible by human standards. It is a state of mind that is possible to reach by adopting broader ways of looking at circumstances while being disciplined about how you conduct your life. You search for a sign of this utopia through external means, only to be consistently left with disappointment. This is because utopia begins and ends inside the spark that burns within your spirit like a pilot light waiting to be ignited.

Living for the Weekend

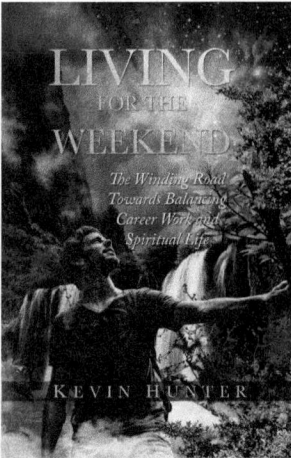

The Winding Road Towards Balancing Career Work and Spiritual Life

Available in Paperback and E-book

Working hard to ensure your bills are paid can leave your soul spiritually starved for soul nourishment. When your ultimate goal is to obtain enough money to be comfortable that you become carried away in that current, then there is little to no room for Divine enrichment.

Many work to survive in jobs they hate because it's the way it is. As a result, they experience and endure all sorts of emotional pain whether it is through depression, sadness, anger, or any other kind of negative stressor. Some silently suffer through this emotional strain gradually killing off their life force. If you don't have a healthy social life and positive fun filled activities and hobbies to balance that burden outside of that, then that could add additional tension. What's it all for if you can't live the life you've always wanted to live? Instead, you spend your days growing forever miserable and broken.

Living for the Weekend examines the pitfalls, struggles, as well as the benefits available in the current modern day working world. This is followed up with spiritual and practical tips, guidance, messages, and discussions on ways to incorporate more balance and enlightenment to a cutthroat material driven world.

MONSTERS
AND ANGELS

An Empath's Guide to Finding Peace in a Technologically Driven World Ripe with Toxic Monsters and Energy Draining Vampires

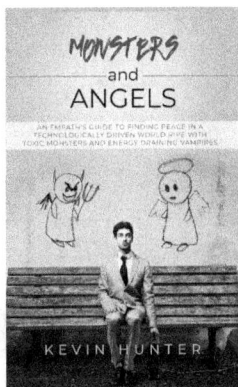

Every person on the planet is capable of being empathic and sensitive, to becoming an energy vampire or toxic monster. No one is exempt from displaying the darker sides of their ego. The easiest and most efficient way to spread any kind of energy is online. Every time you log onto the Internet, there is a larger chance you're going to see something related to the news, media, or gossip areas thrown in front of you, even if you attempt to avoid it as much as possible. You're absorbing everything that your consciousness faces, including the ugly and the wicked, which has its own consequences. This tempestuous energy is tossed into the Universe ultimately creating a flame-throwing battleground inside and around you.

Monsters and Angels discusses how technology, media, and social media have an immense power in distributing both positive and negative influences far and wide. This is about being mindful of what can negatively affect your state of being, and how to counter and avoid that when and wherever possible. This is why it's beneficial to govern yourself, your life, and your surroundings like a strict disciplined executive.

Twin Flame Soul Connections

*Recognizing the Split Apart, the Truths and Myths of Twin Flames,
Soul Love Connections, Soul Mates, and Karmic Relationships*

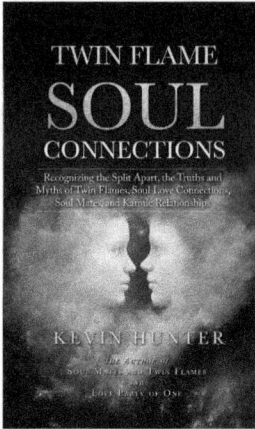

Twin Flames have a shared ongoing sentiment and quest from the moment they're a spark shooting out of God's love that explodes into a blinding white fire that breaks apart causing one to be two, until two become one again, separate and whole, and back around again. Looking into the eyes of your Twin Flame is like looking into the eyes of God, because to know love is to know God.

When one thinks of a Soul Mate or Twin Flame, they might equate it to a passionate romantic relationship where you're making love on a white sandy palm tree lined beach in paradise for the rest of your lives. This beautiful mythological notion has caused great turmoil in others who long for this person that fits the description of a lothario character in a romance novel. It is also an unrealistic and misguided interpretation of the Soul Mate or Twin Flame dynamic.

Twin Flame Soul Connections discusses and lists some of the various myths and truths surrounding the Twin Flames, and how to identify if you've come into contact with your Twin Flame, or if you know someone who has. The ultimate goal is not to find ones Twin Flame, but to awaken ones heart to love, and to work on becoming complete and whole as an individual soul through spiritual self-mastery, life lessons, growth, and raising your consciousness. Your soul's life was born out of love and will die right back into that love.

IGNITE YOUR INNER LIFE FORCE

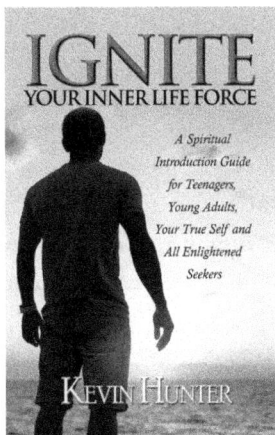

Ignite Your Inner Life Force is an introduction guide for teens, young adults, and anyone seeking answers, messages, and guidance and surrounding spiritual empowerment. This is from understanding what Heaven, the soul, and spiritual beings are to knowing when you are connecting with your Spirit team of Guides and Angels. Some of the topics covered are communicating with Heaven, working with your Spirit team, what your higher self is, your life purpose and soul contract, what the ego is, love and relationships, your vibration energy, shifting your consciousness and thinking for yourself even when you stand alone. This is an in-depth primer manual offering you foundation as you find a higher purpose navigating through your personal journey in today's modern day practical world.

AWAKEN YOUR CREATIVE SPIRIT

Your creative spirit is more than being artistic and getting involved in creativity pursuits, although this is a good part of it. When your creative spirit is activated by a high vibration state of being, then this is the space you create from. You can apply this to your dealings in life, your creative and artistic pursuits, and to having a greater communication line with your Spirit team on the Other Side. *Awaken Your Creative Spirit* is an overview of what it means to have access to Divine assistance and how that plays a part in arousing the muse within you in order to bring your state of mind into a happier space.

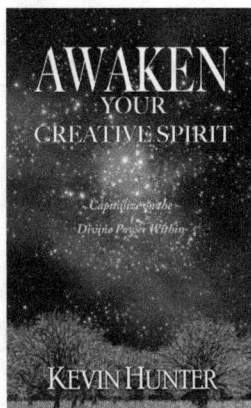

The *Warrior of Light* series of pocket books are available in paperback and E-book called, *Spirit Guides and Angels, Soul Mates and Twin Flames, Divine Messages for Humanity, Raising Your Vibration, Connecting with the Archangels*, and *The Seven Deadly Sins*

TAROT CARD MEANINGS

A Beginner's Guide to the
FOUR PSYCHIC CLAIR SENSES

Learn about the four main psychic clair senses to help you connect with Heaven, the Spirit World, and the Other Side. Take that one step further and use those senses to read the Tarot! *Tarot Card Meanings* is an encyclopedia reference guide that takes the Tarot apprentice reader through each of the 78 Tarot Cards offering the potential general meanings and interpretations that could be applied when conducting a reading, whether it be spiritual, love, general, or work related questions. This is an easy to understand manual for the Tarot novice that is having trouble interpreting cards for themselves, or a Tarot reader who loves the craft and is looking for a refresher or another point of view. The *Four Psychic Clair Senses* focuses on the main channels that Heaven and Spirit communicate with you. *Both books are available in Paperback and E-book wherever books are sold.*

Available in Paperback and E-Book
is the B-Side to the Attracting in Abundance book

ABUNDANCE ENLIGHTENMENT
An Easy Motivational Guide to
the Laws of Attracting in Abundance
and Transforming Your Soul

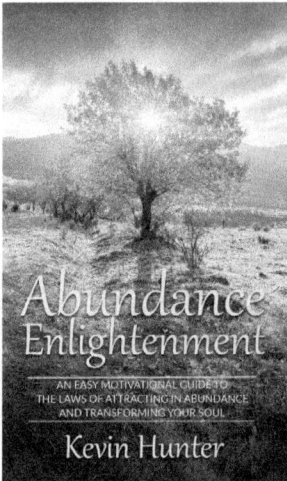

Ultimate authentic success surrounds your soul's growth and evolving process. It's when you realize that none of the physical ego driven desires matter in the end. You can work hard to make sure you stay afloat, you're able to pay your bills, and support yourself and family, but you're not chasing popularity for external validation. Any amount of goodness displayed from your heart is the true measure of real accomplishment.

An overflowing feeling of optimism and love coupled with faith and action is what increases the chances of attracting good things and positive experiences to you. Abundance is more than monetary and financial increase. It can also be about reaching an optimistic well-being state of joy, peace, and love. This positive emotional mindful state simultaneously attracts in blessings.

Abundance Enlightenment is the follow up book to *Attracting in Abundance*. It contains both practical guidance and spirit wisdom that can be applied to everyday life. Some of the key topics surround the laws of attraction as well as healthier money management and improving your soul to help make you a fine tuned in abundance attractor.

About Kevin Hunter

Kevin Hunter is the metaphysical spiritual author of more than two-dozen spiritually based books that tackle a variety of genres and tend to have a strong male protagonist. The messages and themes he weaves in his work surround Spirit's own communications of love and respect, which he channels and infuses into his writing work.

His spiritually based empowerment books include *Warrior of Light, Empowering Spirit Wisdom, Realm of the Wise One, Reaching for the Warrior Within, Darkness of Ego, Transcending Utopia, Living for the Weekend, Ignite Your Inner Life Force, Awaken Your Creative Spirit,* and *Tarot Card Meanings.* His metaphysical pocket books series include, *Spirit Guides and Angels, Soul Mates and Twin Flames, Raising Your Vibration, Divine Messages for Humanity, Connecting with the Archangels, The Seven Deadly Sins, Four Psychic Clair Senses, Monsters and Angels, Twin Flame Soul Connections, Attracting in Abundance,* and *Abundance Enlightenment.* He is also the author of the dating singles guide *Love Party of One,* the horror/drama, *Paint the Silence,* and the modern day erotic love story, *Jagger's Revolution.*

Kevin started out in the entertainment business in 1996 as the personal development guy to one of Hollywood's most respected talent, Michelle Pfeiffer, for her boutique production company, Via Rosa Productions. She dissolved her company after several years and he made a move into coordinating film productions for the studios on such films as *One Fine Day, A Thousand Acres, The Deep End of the Ocean, Crazy in Alabama, The Perfect Storm, Original Sin, Harry Potter & the Sorcerer's Stone, Dr. Dolittle 2,* and *Carolina.* He considers himself a beach bum born and raised in Southern California. For more information: www.kevin-hunter.com

CPSIA information can be obtained
at www.ICGtesting.com
Printed in the USA
LVHW081710200120
644181LV00039B/2624

9 780615 922355